What a Hunter Brings Home

Steve Chapman

HARVEST HOUSE PUBLISHERS
Eugene, Oregon 97402

Cover by Paz Design Group, Salem, Oregon

Cover photo by Charles J. Alsheimer

Back cover photo by Eddy Richey

WHAT A HUNTER BRINGS HOME
Copyright © 2000 by Paul Stephen Chapman (text and illustrations)
Published by Harvest House Publishers
Eugene, Oregon 97402

Library of Congress Cataloging-in-Publication Data
Chapman, Steve
    What a hunter brings home / Steve Chapman
        p. cm.
    ISBN 0-7369-0441-7
        1. Hunting—Anecdotes. 2. Chapman, Steve. I. Title.
SK33.C48 2001
799.2—dc21   00-056697

Printed in the United States of America.

01   02   03   04   05   06   / BP-CF /   10   9   8   7   6   5   4   3

To my sweet wife,

Annie,

who most appreciates what I bring

home from the hunter's woods.

I love her with all my heart.

Contents

Enduring
Encounters

There's a room upstairs in our house that is rarely occupied. It's Nathan's bedroom where, except on occasions such as spring break or Christmas vacation, the bed stays nicely made and the floor is uncluttered with his clothes and college textbooks. In that quiet room, on the top of a wall of bookshelves, is an artful mount of a big fox squirrel. In its permanent running pose it looks intently at whoever enters its territory. And, without saying a word, it tells the tale of the late afternoon many years ago when a father watched his young son meet with success in the hunter's woods. The preserved bushytail is one of our most valued treasures.

In a room farther down the hall, there is another walled creature. It is Nathan's very first deer—a six-point. It hangs above a little work table where I often go for the therapeutic activity of painting and drawing. Each time I enter the room and see the whitetail's sleek features, I am called back to the November day in 1991 when the big event happened. This mount is also among our most prized possessions.

I have no doubt that on countless walls in myriad homes across America are mounted memories just like Nathan's "big red" and his buck. And most of us know these testimonies to successful hunts do not come cheap. However, the investment always seems worth it just after the kill when the buzz of adrenaline is still affecting the brain. Of course, when six months pass and the phone call announces that the taxidermist has completed his work, I sometimes wonder how many of us cringe at the thought of forking out the big bucks for the preserved furry creatures. Fortunately, the salve for the financial wound we inflict on ourselves is applied when we show up at the shop and reconnect with the trophy. In most cases, we are not disappointed in the investment.

What is this strange ritual of letting these silent, ghostly figures loom above us in our dwellings? I have to admit that if someone stopped to think about the idea of taking dead animals and stuffing them and hanging them on his or her wall, it would seem rather odd. It must be especially difficult to accept for those who are squeamish when it comes to taking the life of a deer, squirrel, turkey, duck, or any other critter. This feeling is understandable.

While these displays may seem crude and even barbaric to some, I believe they are surprisingly more significant than people realize. Somewhere deep in the recesses of the hearts of today's hunters is a desire to bring something home that is more than just food. We have an intense longing to show our ability to conquer. In this age of technology, when the challenging quests that some of us face hardly go beyond getting up on time for a regular job, hunting a highly elusive animal presents a tangible opportunity to rise above the mundane.

For those who are aware of the ratio between how many times hunters go afield compared to how rarely they go home with a harvest, the opportunity to exhibit the evidence of a hunting achievement makes sense. One year, for example, I hunted whitetail deer in both archery and firearm seasons, on 30 different days, and the outcome was only one load of venison for the freezer. That result is indicative of who usually wins during the "wild game" adventure.

In addition to the successful conquest that a mount represents, there is another wonderful accomplishment it signifies. In most cases, an incredible memory made with a family member or friend is stirred each time we look at our walls. The feelings that wash over the soul when these recollections return are warm and welcome. Very often the memory of the hunt that resulted in the animal that graces a room carries with it something that will last for ages. The huge squirrel on Nathan's shelf, for example, may be lifeless, but the joy of the time we spent together lives on. Truth is, that lone squirrel stands for many other days we ventured out when a gun was never fired. The trips alone triggered a lot of good conversations. Most importantly, we carried out of the woods a closer bond as father and son. In my estimation, trophies just don't come any bigger and better than that.

There is one other by-product that our "wall-hangers" symbolize. When we as individuals face the odds that nature often throws at us, there is always something eternal that can be gleaned from the experience. Of course, this can be true only if the hunter is looking for it. Too many people go headlong into the wild not aware that along with the animals they pursue there are valuable insights about body, soul, and spirit that can be found. A lot of us, however, have learned to go hunting with the expectation that we will encounter something that can change our very characters or at least send us back to our loved ones a little bit improved.

The pages that follow are a collection of adventures in the hunter's woods that resulted in success. While some trophies had fur or feathers and can now be seen in a couple of rooms in our house, others hang only on the walls of my heart. It is my hope that if you are a person who loves the outdoors, the familiar ring in the stories will strike a harmonious chord in you. If, on the other hand, you are one who looks tentatively at those of us who embrace the challenge of a fair chase, it is my sincere desire that this reading will reveal to you an undeniable fact: It does not matter if our game bag is full or empty when we leave the woods. There is always something valuable in what a hunter brings home.

1

The Petrich Method

More than five years have passed since my son and I made our way to the incredible state of Montana to hunt the mighty elk. We had planned and anticipated the experience with such a high level of excitement that it made the weeks and days prior to our departure seem to crawl by like a snail with a bad limp.

Even though we were scheduled for only five days of hunting, for me the hunt actually spanned several months. From the day I committed to the trip the previous year, those handful of October mornings and evenings that we were to spend in the Livingston area occupied my thoughts day and night. I was consumed with making the necessary plans to ensure a successful trip. Having never hunted in the type of territory we were going into and not really knowing exactly how to prepare, I filled several pages with notations of what to take, what to do to get ready, and what budget was necessary regarding needed purchases. While the pull of the trigger on our .270s would last only one intensely exciting moment, getting to that point was a journey I managed to make long and enjoyable.

Having so much time to prepare, however, had an unexpected consequence. It didn't reveal itself until Nathan and I dismounted our horses, Dan and Spook, that first morning at the base of a towering Montana mountain. Within a few minutes after falling in behind our guide, Randy Petrich, I knew we were in trouble. Randy, founder of Rising Son Outfitters, was in his mid- to late-twenties at that time and was raised on the property we were hunting. He had an untold number of climbs under the belt that circled his very fit waist. His strong legs reached for each step with a vigor that was nothing less than frightening. About 100 yards up the trail, Nathan and I looked at each other in the pale, predawn darkness with a certain horror. It was the kind of look that says, "Repent—for soon you will die!"

The kind of effort that was suddenly required of our Tennessee flatland legs left us gasping for breath. Though we had made an attempt at getting in shape before October arrived, our lungs burned, our eyes watered, our calves pulsed, and a disconcerting sweat began to form under our stocking caps. We clutched our rifles and dug the toes of our boots into the dirt and fought to keep up with Randy. I whispered a prayer that our loved ones would not be too saddened when they heard how our hearts had exploded from over-exertion.

What's worse is that all those months of notes I had written regarding equipment needed for the hunt were translated from paper to our backpacks, pockets, and fanny packs. The weight of it all added to the burden of being half in-shape. Here's what we had:

Liquids. In addition to carrying enough water to irrigate the enormous wheat fields we had crossed earlier that morning on horseback, I threw in a couple cans of pop for each of us just for variety.

Food. Let the party begin!

Clothing. An extra set of dry uppers and lowers, as well as extra footwear in the packs. It looked like a Cabelas warehouse back there.

Ammo. Thirty rounds each. You never know when a war might break out!

Miscellaneous items. Cameras, rope, flashlights, knives, extra batteries, small radio, small alarm clock (Not kidding! Wouldn't want to nap through the evening hunt), tracking ribbon, the "Good Book" for midday breaks, rain gear, a space-age survival blanket, binoculars, and by all means…toilet paper.

Medical supplies. Everything from aspirin to emergency cold compresses for my aging and injured knees. Band-Aids, moleskin for the feet, salves, cleansing agents, and other items were tightly stored somewhere in the bottom of my sack. I was ready for any catastrophe. As my heart rate soared to uncharted regions for a man in midlife, the only other thing I was wishing I had packed was a wheelchair. I was sure I would need it.

Only 200 yards into a hike that would turn out to be well over 2.5 miles, I was seriously rethinking the strategy I had followed in packing for the hunt. As a stream of sweat ran down my right temple and dripped onto my already aching shoulder, I was tempted to do something rash. I thought about dumping everything but my rifle and a couple of bullets. It was the same temptation faced by many of the Appalachian Trail (AT) "through hikers." As they head up that first mountain in the southern state of Georgia in early May to begin conquering the 2150-mile snake that runs to Maine, they do something really strange. They go through a shedding ritual. It's a nearly ceremonial exercise of casting off expensive gear. I've heard if a person wants to equip themselves at no cost with every conceivable piece of hiking and camping equipment known to mankind, just go to the trailhead of the AT in Georgia. There, as you ascend Springer Mountain, it is said that you will find everything from portable stoves to high-tech tents. These items are thrown away by those who realized within that first painful, uphill mile that if the long path ahead of them was to be defeated, they could not proceed under such heavy burdens. As a result, valuable items they thought they would definitely need quickly paled in comparison to their longing for lighter loads. Thus, they say, Springer Mountain is the place to shop!

I began to mentally plunder my pack and consider what I could leave behind. I knew Nathan had to be feeling some level of resentment at his old dad's overdone plan. While I fought to put one foot in front of the other, I was shortening my list of needs. The fact that we weren't terribly far from the horses made the idea of leaving some stuff by the trail seem more attractive by the minute. *It would be easy to find,* I thought. *We couldn't possibly miss a five-foot-high pile of gear, even in the dark.*

As I was about to pull the cord and stop the human train that was puffing up the mountain, I suddenly ran headlong into Randy's back. I had been looking down and must've been praying for mercy when we collided. I apologized for plowing into our young guide, and he just sort of quietly laughed. He didn't say anything at all as he turned from looking at us and stared straight ahead. I thought at first he saw a grizzly or some other hungry monster up on the trail. As I stood there waiting for him to yell, "Run!" I noticed his breathing was normal. He wasn't even the least bit winded. "That's disgusting!" I muttered to myself. Nathan and I, on the other hand, sounded like a couple of hand saws cutting through oak. We just couldn't get enough of that clear, thin air into our lungs that were on fire.

After about 45 seconds of just standing conversationless on the trail, Randy took off again. There was a spring in his step that was disturbing.

Two hundred yards later, he did it again. He suddenly halted and stood with one foot further up the hill than the other. Nathan and I put on the brakes and thanked our Maker that we were still upright. We were grateful for the break.

A third time, after the same distance was covered, Randy stopped again. This time he turned to us and asked, "You guys O.K.?" We didn't respond with words. We just grunted an affirmative. Actually, by doing so, we both lied. *We were not O.K.!* But neither of us were about to admit it. No way! We didn't want our cautious host to think we might have to go back. Instead, we looked at each other with that "don't let Mr. Randy-the-gazelle-guide think we're pansies" look. Without saying anything to one another, my hurting son and I decided that we would keep up with him even if it damaged our brains (and we were closer to that state than we wanted to admit).

Somehow 30 minutes passed and Nathan and I were still among the living. Also, we were well into our second mile. As the mountain began to receive the morning gift of light from the east, it suddenly dawned on me why we were able to get as far as we did without throwing our cargo overboard. It was a result of what Nathan and I came to call "the Petrich Method." If we were to draw a line from where we were at that moment back to the horses and put a mark at each place Randy Petrich had stopped us for a timely rest, the marks would be equidistant from each other at about 200-yard intervals. I could see the pattern. Climb, rest a minute, climb, rest a minute, and so on. That's how we had done it. Somehow those 45- to 60-second reprieves were all we needed. They allowed us to catch our breaths, recover, and ward off impending doom. They were "power breaks."

I was convinced, though I never did ask Randy if it was true, that his method of gingerly leading "soft" hunters up that mountainside came about as a result of years of listening to the noises made by hurting hunters. Coughing, gurgling, gasping, and vomiting are surefire signs that someone needs a break. Besides, none of that is good for an elk hunt. Foreign sounds and odors can really mess up an exciting pursuit of the highly sensitive elk.

By the time the first day had ended, we not only accomplished a healthy climb, we also put the stalk on a couple of potential "freezer fillers." Though our tags were not filled out when sunset came, we did have the trophy of confidence that when the end of day five rolled around we would be able to say we had conquered the mountains. We both knew it could be done as long as Randy utilized his wise climbing technique designed for Easterners like us.

Back at the camp, after a great supper at Dena's table, we laid our sore bodies down in the "bunkhouse." And, believe it or not, both of us looked forward to the next morning's 4:30 A.M. wake-up call and the muscle massacre we would endure once again on the mountain. On the evening of day two, I met up with a nice 6x6, and Nathan did the same on the fourth day. It was an incredible experience for father and son—and we lived to tell about it. And it could not have been done had Randy not been so kind to our psyches by being gentle on our physiques.

When we returned home, whitetail season was in full swing and our hunting adventures continued. In the fine state of Tennessee, the peaks we must climb are mere bumps compared to the territory we had seen in the West. It was almost humorous to think how quickly we could ascend to the top of our little hills around our county. I even noticed a spring in my steps. It was gratifying.

Since the elk hunt, Nathan and I have had other occasions to practice the Randy Petrich (RP) Method. Some have involved the outdoors. For example, my daughter, Heidi, Nathan, and I went to the Appalachian Trail for a three-day traverse in Great Smoky Mountains National Park. The RP method sure was a blessing. Heidi was especially grateful for the one-minute vacations on the steep climbs. She now loves Mr. Randy, too.

Not all opportunities to employ Randy's endurance technique have been on hillsides filled with forest and foliage. Some have been during grueling travel schedules as I hurriedly trotted through places such as O'Hare International Airport in Chicago burdened with my heavy guitar case and dragging my overstuffed equipment bag. Just to step aside and stop for a brief moment and then continue has helped me arrive at a concert location in a much better frame of mind.

For Nathan and Heidi, it has been during Greek or math classes at college or while facing mountains of homework. It is then that they have enlisted Randy's wisdom. Just to stop, sigh, make a cup of coffee, and look out the window of the dorm can easily make the difference between conquering or conceding a task.

Even Annie, my nonhunting wife, has incorporated Randy's fine method into her life. It was especially important to her as she climbed the emotional mountain of saying farewell to her mother in 1996 and as she and her five siblings cared for their widowed father until he went to be with the Lord two years later.

At this moment, life may be requiring you to endure some type of difficult ascent. Does the climb have you completely exhausted, wondering if you can go on? Whatever the mountain you face, remember Randy Petrich and the picture he gives us of the wisdom found in Psalm 37:7: "Rest in the LORD and wait patiently for Him."

Let God be your guide. He knows when to stop you. He hears when you're gasping for air. He'll know how long to pause, and He'll know when to lead you onward.

2

The White Flag of Victory

Many are the times I've been sneaking through a thicket, quiet as a mountain lion on the prowl, only to have my heart nearly burst through my sternum at the sound of an escaping herd of startled deer. In that moment filled with flying leaves, crashing limbs, and ear-piercing snorts, it's all I can do to keep from passing out.

While it's exciting to catch a glimpse of several of earth's most beautiful and elusive creatures, the sight of four or five whitetails bouncing away like superballs thrown on concrete is depressing. It's a sure sign that I would do well to just go on home. The chances of seeing the group again are about as good as getting to my treestand and finding Elvis sitting there in bell-bottom camouflage pants. (Then again, who knows?)

I suppose there have been a few of us who've thrown an open-sighted rifle to the shoulder and managed to connect with a fast, escaping deer. Of course, the wisdom of that kind of shot is as little as the safety of it. In no way do I recommend spraying lead projectiles into the forest without knowing what is beyond the target. That's just not a smart thing to do. And even though I know it's unsafe and a low-percentage shot, when the whitetails suddenly fill my vision I instinctively try to get one in my sights. Though I never squeeze the trigger, unless one of them stops for a second and gives me a chance to look beyond his position, I realize it is an instinctive reaction that is almost uncontrollable.

In regards to the "flagging" a whitetail deer does when running away, I can't help but wonder why our Creator chose to equip them with such opposing characteristics. On one hoof, deer are incredibly cautious. On the other, they are made highly visible because of the brilliant white fur under their tails. Since it is likely that none of us will fully know God's mind on this matter (until we can ask Him personally), we are left to speculate on the reasons.

Interestingly enough, all the arguments I have heard hold so much logic that it seems each one could be true. Here's a sampling:

1. Throwing up the tail and revealing a mass of bright white tends to momentarily startle and stall a would-be predator, allowing deer to put some needed distance between them and their pursuers. This is often called "flash behavior." Once safely ahead of whatever might be chasing it, the deer will then often stop, drop its tail, and disappear by blending into its surroundings. I've seen this phenomena. It's amazing.

2. Deer in groups speak a silent language to each other with their tails. A flicker while

grazing means they are relaxed. A slow rise indicates a warning to other deer that danger has been detected. A cunning hunter will watch for these signs as deer are moving into his area.

3. The younger of the herd can more easily follow their parents or other adults, especially when an escape is being made.

While I appreciate the common sense in all the above opinions, it will be fine with me if this unique trait of the whitetail continues as a mystery. Though it is likely to remain an unknown, one thing is for certain: When a hunter sees a snow-colored, furry ensign bounding off into the distance, it's likely that the deer prevails and the hunter's tag stays in his or her pocket. It may be true for battles between people that a raised white flag means surrender, but not so for deer. They're saying, "We win!"

As peculiar as this maneuver is to the deer species, I must tell you I have seen a time when the waving of the white flag meant victory among humans, too. I saw it in West Virginia years ago when I was just a kid—and it happened more than once.

The very first person I ever remember using this tactic borrowed from the animal kingdom was my Grandma Steele. I couldn't have been but six, maybe eight years old. We were in a large group of people, and I was sitting between my mom and dad. Grandma was down the row from me with her purse in her lap. A man stepped to the front of the room and started singing E.M. Bartlett's "Victory in Jesus":

O victory in Jesus,
my Savior, forever
He sought me
and bought me
with His redeeming blood.
He loved me ere I knew Him,
and all my love is due Him.
He plunged me to victory
beneath the cleansing flood. *

Suddenly my dignified grandmother reached into her purse, took out a white hankie, and raised it over her head. She began waving it back and forth, all the while voicing a joyous-sounding, high-pitched sob. Then all around the room, one by one, other men and women began to join her. The memory of about 20 white, waving handkerchiefs unfurled and vigorously fluttering overhead remains precious in my heart to this day.

I know now that with their white flags those saints were saying, "We win! Through the victory wrought by the crucified but risen Christ, we win over sin and death!" Though Satan, their worst predator, would have loved it if they raised pale flags of defeat and surrender, they instead lifted pure, white banners of triumph and encouraged each other with their ceremonial waving.

It has been way too long since I've seen a group of Christians celebrate in such a way. I suppose we've come too far for such displays. About the only reason a hankie comes out of a purse or pocket these days is to wipe away the sweat of worry that the brother on the other side of the church

---

* Victory in Jesus by E.M. Bartlett, ©Albert E. Brumley & Sons, c/o Integrated Copyright Group, Nashville, TN. Used by permission.

might say another amen or raise a hand in praise. I wonder what people would do if you tried a little flag-waving some Sunday during communion?

I suppose I'll never see another spray of whitetails in the field again in the same way. As they hurry to escape the danger I represent to them, I will consider their flashing as a sign that I have been conquered. I'll let them bound away in the joy of their conquest. And the next time I'm in church and someone starts singing "Victory in Jesus," I hope I have a white hankie in my pocket.

3

A Divine Breeze

At sunrise there was a calmness in the woods that was unbelievable. Nothing around me was moving. Absolutely nothing. I strained to see if the remnants of a spider web that hung from a nearby branch might show some motion. It was lifeless. I imagined the stillness that surrounded me must be what it is like inside a coffin.

I thought to myself, *This planet is screaming through space at about 66,000 miles per hour as it revolves around the sun. At the same time, it's rotating once every 24 hours. Surely some slight breeze would be stirred up!* Yet the woods were as stationary as a statue. *Where is the wind?*

Nearly 30 minutes of legal shooting light had passed. I had never experienced such an intense calm that clung to the world. It was eerie. The only movements were the rise and fall of my chest as I breathed in the comforting aroma of the forest floor and the silent shifting of my eyes as I carefully scanned the area around me.

Then it happened. As I was looking straight ahead I saw it out of the corner of my right eye. I was tempted to snap my head around and get a look at the source of the motion but I fought the urge. *Be patient,* I begged myself.

The movement was slight and sort of dainty. My heart raced. I mentally prepared for action. Without moving my head, I looked down at my bow and slowly attached the release to the string. Every effort to get ready for a long-awaited shot at a whitetail had to be unhurried and deliberate. One slight ping or clank of metal on metal, or any unnatural sound, and the hunt would be over. To a deer's sensitive ear, even the subdued scraping of my arrow across the vinyl-coated pronged rest would sound like fingernails on a chalkboard in the intense silence of the morning.

When I finally had the release in place and a little bit of tension on the string I decided to turn my head about three inches to the right. Forcing my eyes as far as they could toward the movement, which I could still detect in my peripheral vision, I slowly rotated my face toward my right shoulder. My eyes watered with excitement, and I could almost taste the adrenaline as my heart pounded in anticipation. Every natural inclination in my body was screaming for me to stand up, turn completely around, and come to full draw. The battle was fierce but wisdom was winning. I assumed that within a few seconds I would get a view of the four-legged creature I had come to meet.

It seemed like five minutes before I finally connected visually with my soon to be trophy. There it was! Colorful. Mature. Totally unaware of my presence. As I took in the sight of my target, my racing heart ran out of fuel and coasted to a dead stop. My emotions drained from me like water out of a sink. My muscles that were as rigid as steel became as limp as wet noodles. Why? Because the movement was that of one lone leaf, leaping merrily on the morning thermal that was beginning to rise from the forest floor. I muttered the words that had been branded into my mind back in the 60s: *"What a bummer!"*

I looked beyond the happy little leaf hoping to see a tail of white out there in the woods. I desperately wanted there to be a lifeform other than the one that had captured my full attention and sucked a gallon of nature's stimulant from my system. Nothing was there, and I had to face the truth. I had been snookered by a dancing leaf!

Gratified only by the fact that I had seen it without it first seeing me, I turned my head back to its original position and restarted my search for a creature that had blood flowing through its veins instead of chlorophyll. I turned my face over my left shoulder and checked the ridgeline trail that passed nearby. Nothing was there. I watched it for several minutes, focusing primarily on a canopy of brush that formed a cavelike cover over the well-worn path. I had seen deer walk right through it on other days, and I began imagining a nicely antlered, unsuspecting buck walking under it as it browsed on the fruit of the white oak. For three or four minutes my big buck fantasies ran wild. The daydreams were therapeutic because I was gradually returning to the hopeful state of mind that had been stolen a few minutes earlier by the trickery of nature.

Before looking forward again, I turned my body slightly to the left to get a peek directly behind my treestand. The view was furless, so I rotated my head to look in front of me. When my face locked in straight my side vision caught the glimpse of motion to my right. My eyes suddenly widened, and my heart began to flutter once more. I could feel my body wanting to constrict every muscle as the intense excitement rushed through me. *Oh! The joy of it all! This is why I'm here!* I thought.

Then it hit me. Like someone who had just heard those famous words that are mischievously uttered on the first day of April. I realized that for the second time in only a few short minutes, I had been completely fooled. The little yellowish-white dangling menace had been successful once again at draining the optimism from my spirit. I felt defeated and embarrassed.

I would like to say that it didn't happen again that morning. Unfortunately, there were more lapses of memory and hopes repeatedly dashed on the rocks of disappointment. It was as if I couldn't remember from one episode to the next. I was having some serious "senior moments"! It was disturbing. It would not be good for my reputation to reveal the exact number of times I actually heard that solitary leaf say to me, "Made you look!"

I was getting quite perturbed by it all. I was tempted to dismount my stand, walk over to the leaf that swayed jovially about six feet off the ground, pinch its little petiole between my thumb and index finger, and snap it off at the bud. Then I would eat the silly thing because I figured I wouldn't be taking anything else home for the freezer that day.

But I stayed put. It was far too much trouble to climb down and then ascend the tree again. I decided to just let the stupid thing do its jig and wish for a weakening of its connection to the limb. Then, if it let go and plunged to its death, I would find sweet revenge in its falling.

As I sat there, eyes straight ahead and now nearly able to find the humor in my ongoing battle with the distraction of the leaping leaf, I suddenly thought of something that made the entire skirmish worthwhile. The notion that came to me switched my feelings from disdain for the leaf to an appreciation for what it represented.

"At daylight," I reminded myself, "there was a calm about these woods that was almost spooky. The unusual stillness was nearly a threat to the joy of the solitude. Then, as the ever so slight current of wind gently rose off the warming ground, it began to drift upward and the leaf felt it. No other object around it responded. It unashamedly began to rock gracefully back and forth as if it alone was willing to announce to the rest of creation, 'Something unseen is among us!' But as it was giving itself completely to the effect of the breeze, it couldn't know that nearby was an enemy that had a heart filled with rage at its frolicking. What was making it happy was making me mad. It was tormenting me to see it living. That leaf was a major distraction!"

I can see a reflection of my life in that leaf, especially if I apply a passage found in the second chapter of Ephesians:

> And you were dead in your trespasses and sins....But God, being rich in mercy, because of His great love with which He loved us...made us alive together with Christ...and raised us up with Him...so that in the ages to come He might show the surpassing riches of His grace in kindness toward us in Christ Jesus. For by grace you have been saved through faith; and that not of yourselves, it is the gift of God (verses 1,4-8).

Like that motionless leaf at daylight, my spirit once had no life, no movement. Then, when Christ was raised from the dead and the gentle, warm current of His kind Spirit began to blow across the earth, it eventually touched me and I responded by accepting Him. The result? My spirit couldn't help but dance in His divine breeze. And when it did, my new life became a distraction to my friends.

As my changing character began to show the effects of the wind of the Holy Spirit, those who were hunting for the pleasures of this present world were troubled each time they saw me. I was a reminder to them that something other than what they were hoping to find was making me content. I was different. I became someone to ignore, even hate. Yet I danced. I couldn't tell they were disowning me. All I could do was dance. I didn't recognize their looks of rejection. I was dancing. I didn't hear their unkind words. I was caught up in a divine current. The Wind had found me, and I was leaping with it. I was alive—and it was tormenting them.

As I sat in my treestand that morning, I recalled the name of one particular person from my distant past who seemed to have most resented my conversion to Christ. I remembered how much he desperately wanted to "pluck me off the vine," to bring a quick end to the distraction I had become to him. He tried more than once to call me back to lifelessness. Fortunately, Christ hung on to me and I didn't fall.

I had long since lost touch with him, and I wondered where he was and if he had ever responded to the "Holy Thermal." As I stared at the lone witness that danced in midair nearby, I quietly prayed, *Lord, if my old friend hasn't allowed You to do it already, may You give him the courage to let You do for him what You did for me. Make him a leaping leaf!*

4

"He Walked Here!"

In all honesty, as one who passionately loves the pursuit of the whitetail deer, I can't say that I am a "rack hunter." Instead, I consider my primary purpose in the enjoyable challenge of deer hunting to be the harvest of a great source of meat. From one average-size doe here in Tennessee, the yield can be well over 40 pounds of boned, tasty venison. That proportion cannot be found in a single carcass of a smaller species, such as squirrel or turkey, even though the animal or bird may be preferred for the table. I venture to say that it would take at least 10 to 15 turkeys to equal one deer in terms of volume of meat. I appreciate the economy of the kill when it comes to comparisons between whitetail and the rest of the legally hunted, edible animals.

Furthermore, in my experience, the overall taste of doe meat is generally better. I'll admit that early archery season males can be less "gamey," but after an old buck has been whipped by the rut and is drenched with the hormones that drive him crazy, it requires far too much spice to cover the wild taste. If the goal is to see the smiles on the faces of family and friends as they sit with their feet under my supper table and take in the animal I worked hard at harvesting, then bringing home an antlered deer can be risky. Besides, no matter how thin you slice them, no matter how long you boil them, antlers never soften up. A fellow can break a tooth gnawing on a tine.

If my position on this issue were a sermon, it would be entitled, "The Virtue of Going Antlerless!" It is a message I have preached for years. When I see the covers of hunting magazines that exclusively feature the trophy bucks and their rocking-chair-sized antlers, it makes me wonder if the overemphasis on the big, bruiser bucks only furthers the notion that does are not worthy of our time and skills as hunters. Perpetuating this attitude in the media has the dangerous potential of sending the wrong message. Consequently, many immature hunters feel less than accepted and successful if they fail to connect with an antlered deer. The harmful result can be that far too many spikes that would have grown to be well-antlered adults are killed merely for the sake of saying, "I got a buck!" Where is the wisdom in that?

These are the feelings I strongly held onto. Then...one day it happened! Something took place in a recent season that fiercely tampered with my convictions. I confess that I was sorely tempted to retire from the pulpit where I have sermonized about the dangerous doctrine of "rack worship." What happened?...*I saw him!*

I took my son, Nathan, who was home from college, to a stand I had prepared along the edge of a massive, cut soybean field. He faced south, and I was just across a small creek facing north watching a smaller meadow. I was not toting a weapon since my goal was to help Nathan fill a tag. The wind was blowing across us, and the sun was peeking over the horizon.

Suddenly, at about 100 yards to my right in the openness of the field I was monitoring, I saw a deer approaching that I can only describe as…uh…well…diabolical.

If my belief that hunting primarily for meat was a virtue, then I must confess I sinned and did it big time! His body seemed twice the size of any of the three "slickheads" I had already sent to the processor. And atop his head was the most beautiful, perfect set of antlers I had seen in a long, long time. They must have boasted at least a total of ten points. His gait was confident and majestic as he walked.

I whistled softly to Nathan to sneak across the creek and join me. The buck, without knowing we were nearby, turned 90 degrees and headed toward the timber on the far side of the field. Nathan arrived at my side just in time to scope the heavy deer and get a fleeting glimpse of its head gear. All the while I had him in my binoculars, and I must admit that my heart had nearly stopped.

The massive and obviously dominant buck disappeared into the high grass and brushy edge of the woods. The two of us, still shaking, sat motionless, hoping he would reappear further down the field. After about 30 minutes of wishful waiting we resigned ourselves to the likelihood that he was gone for good.

I had hunted that farm for several years and had not seen the size of deer I had suddenly encountered. I'm not sure where he came from, but his arrival spelled trouble for me. For the rest of the season I became a…forgive me…rack hunter. My tightly wound philosophy about being mostly a food hunter came completely unraveled by the sight of the stately creature. My nights were filled with dreams about him. The days when I couldn't sit somewhere on that farm and watch for him were hard to endure. I longed to see him again. I was pitiful!

Perhaps the meeting with such a wondrously gorgeous animal had an alternate purpose besides squelching my excessive pride about being satisfied with doe hunting. For one thing, I began to acquire a new appreciation for those who have an unbridled passion for taking bucks with record-book potential. Because of my "rendezvous with greatness," I was able to pull off the road of resentment and embrace their quest.

Second, I had a good start toward understanding hunters who key in on one huge deer. These folks have some serious challenges to contend with. They are the ones who, for example, sit in church pews on Sunday mornings wishing they could be listening to the sermon by cellphone as they monitored a scrape on some distant ridge. As the pastor pours his heart out with the text from a sermon he labored over for days, the hunter of a specific and massive buck is sitting there in a trance. He may look like he's intently listening to his preacher, but in his mind he's thinking, *If I set up on the north side of that thicket and let the wind work for me, I'll have a better chance when he comes in to bed down. Then again, he's got to be hungry now that the rut is winding down. If I set up in the evening along that winter wheat field, maybe I'll see him as he's coming out to graze!* Thoughts about a big buck consume him. Suddenly the obsessed hunter returns to reality when his wife elbows him sharply in the ribs and announces, "Hey! They asked you to pray the benediction! Wake up, Bubba!"

I am now able to sympathize with this man all because of one brief sighting of the animal he dreams about. If for no other reason than that, it was a good season even though it ended without another glimpse of "my buck." I can only hope he survived the eyes, arrows, and bullets of other hunters. Maybe next year!

Besides seeing the buck that occupied my attention so intensely, the most memorable part of trying to track him again was discovering the sign he left behind. His "scrapes" were broad and the licking branches were high. His rubs destroyed some young cedar trees that were well beyond sapling stage. The does in the area seemed extra skittish, and the young males were a bit more nervous.

But of all the signs that revealed the big buck's presence, his hoofprints were the most telltale evidence of his enormous stature. I dare say one hoof would cover a good portion of this page. It was deep and wide. I guessed his weight to be in the neighborhood of 200 to 230 pounds. The sight of his tracks alone did more to lead this meat hunter astray than any of the other markings that bore witness to his existence. I memorized them. I studied them. And I wanted him!

One day as I walked beside a line he had taken from one side of a plowed field to the other, probably just the night before, the thought came to my mind, *He walked here!* The mystique of being on the very ground that the great beast had occupied just hours before was overwhelming. I stopped and dropped to my knees in the dirt. I spread my index and middle fingers apart about two-and-a-half inches and slipped them down into the depression left by the buck and said again, "He walked here!" I was mesmerized by the connection I felt to that deer. It was a sobering moment.

As I remained in a kneeling position and took in the size of the tracks, I suddenly had one of those thoughts that cross not just the mind, but the heart as well. "Just as these prints testify to the presence of that majestic buck on the earth, there are signs on this great planet that provide proof that God has been, and is, among us. I whispered the revelation audibly but softly, "*He* walked here!"

I began to think of the deep and impressive tracks He had left to reveal His presence. They can be found in the lives of men and women, even hunters. In my heart, where there had once been only darkness and confusion, there was the light of His great love and the clear understanding that He had purchased my salvation through the work of His Son, Jesus. That sign of Him having been among us left a deep, permanent impression in my spirit. And I thought of the children God had given to Annie and me. I was there in the delivery room when they were born. To witness the unbelievable miracle of birthing a human life left an indelible mark on my heart and is one that definitely testifies that "*He* walked here!"

As I scanned the field of my heart, I saw other signs of His having passed by. There in the soil of my flesh was a small scar located on the index finger of my right hand. It was left there by an eight-inch meat cleaver when I was just a child. My Grandpa Chapman was cutting a watermelon with his sharp butchering tool and after he sliced one piece, I reached for it. At that very same moment he came down with the heavy cleaver to cut the second slice and it intercepted my hand that was at the top of the melon, burying it into the lower portion of the rind. When I pulled my hand back I thought I would find a bloody stub. Fortunately, the soft melon had cushioned the blow enough to result only in a severe cut across the outside of my finger. God knew my future would include the guitar and that I would need all my digits. The scar is, in my opinion, a track left there by a loving and merciful God.

God walked here! The phrase echoed in my head as I stood and looked toward the timber. I peered at the edge of the field for a moment then lifted my eyes toward the sky. The words floated freely toward heaven, "Thank You, Father, for reminding me through the big buck that roams in this territory and whose tracks I stand beside that because of the signs You have left in my life, I can assuredly say to others, "He walked here!"

Today I am a convert. Though I still firmly believe that a doe is a wonderful trophy, I can also say that I am now a rack hunter...but for more reasons than just the antlers!

5

"Are You Sure, Dad?"

The game was squirrel. The players: Nathan and I, a father and a son. The stakes were high. If the critter won we would go home empty-handed. If we won, supper was served. The bushytail in the distance was the only one we had seen that evening, and the sun was headed to its hiding place behind the trees.

Nathan was a young outdoorsman, about 11 years old at the time. He was fresh out of the Hunter's Safety course and a novice at handling a gun. But he had shown great aptitude in learning the skills necessary to a be a responsible participant in the hunter's woods. In fact, I was so impressed with how quickly he understood the rules of the game that I surprised him with a challenge as we sat against the big oak and watched the solitary squirrel on a limb about 50 yards away.

"Nathan," I whispered, "see if you can sneak over close enough to get a shot at that squirrel." His youthful eyes widened when he heard my offer. He knew very well that the stealth required to get within range of the skittish critter was reserved for more mature woodsmen. With a look that seemed to question my good judgment, he asked, "Are you sure, Dad? If we're gonna take something home this evening, don't you think you ought to go after him?"

I could hear two feelings in his voice. The first was the hopefulness that I would not withdraw the challenge. His excited demeanor as he answered told me he cherished the prospect of bagging a squirrel on his own. How well I remember the first time I sat alone in the woods with a friend's 20-gauge/.22 caliber, over-under style single shot. I was an anxious 13 year old. I can still feel the tight grip I had on the wooden stock of the gun as I waited for the sighting of my first squirrel. The thought of being by myself with such a powerful instrument was intensely exciting. It was the day I took a giant step toward manhood.

Though Nathan would be only 20 or so yards from me when he got close enough to shoot, at his age he would feel like he had gone to Montana for the hunt. My heart was filled with joy that he was about to taste the responsibility of independence.

The second emotion I detected in his question was a level of doubt. The slight tremor in his voice informed me that even though he was grateful for the challenge, he wasn't totally sure he could rise to the task. It hit me that he truly did want to know if I thought he could do it. All he needed was a nod of assurance from me. I realized I was his source of confidence. He had little on his own.

I understood his hesitance to attempt something so monumental. After all, I was the fellow who, one Sunday night in my early teens, was on my way to the stage with my mom, my dad, and sister at a church our family was visiting. We were invited to sing and my mother always played the Gibson guitar used to accompany the four of us...until that night. She had taught me the chords she knew and coached me as I played for the family, but only in the privacy of our home. However, when we got up out of our seats and started down the side aisle to make our way to the front of the sanctuary, she suddenly turned around, handed me the guitar, and whispered, "Here. You play it tonight."

My reaction that night was exactly the same Nathan gave when I charged him with the task of "bringing home the bacon." I said to my mother, "Are you sure, Mom?"

I remember the mixture of fear and joy that overwhelmed me. I was afraid my brain would not send the signals to my fingers that were needed to form the G, C, and D chords. I feared failure and making a fool of myself. On the other hand, I was overjoyed at the thought that she deemed me an accomplished enough guitarist to play for the family in public.

We were only a few paces from the steps that would lead us up to the stage area when my mom whispered, "I know you can do it, Steve!" That was all I needed. Our little quartet gathered around the podium, I carefully strummed a G chord, Dad started singing, and we were on our way. I strummed along. It was a scene that took place more than 35 years ago and I haven't stopped playing since. To this day the guitar is one of the main tools of my trade.

Would my mother have presented her young son with so great a challenge if she didn't think he could do it? I seriously doubt it. It would have jeopardized the impact of the song. She believed I was capable enough to do the job. Did I believe Nathan was responsible and skilled enough to go after his prey using such a lethal weapon? Of course I did. Otherwise I would have never suggested he do it.

And do it he did. Though the leaves were dry and crunchy like fresh cornflakes, he slowly turned to begin his stalk. As he leaned forward out of the sitting position to get onto all fours, I said, "Son, if you get close, don't forget that when you draw a bead on that squirrel you'll probably get so excited it might be tough to hold steady. If you let yourself get too rattled, you'll miss the shot. You've gotta control yourself. You can win the battle against your nerves. You have to be in charge of them in order to hit your mark."

With that little speech he crawled away. I watched him and also kept an eye on the squirrel that was sitting on a limb working on a hickory nut, silhouetted against the sky. Nathan kept his movements slow and deliberate, producing minimal sound in the noisy leaves. Within three or four minutes he had significantly closed the gap between himself and the squirrel. My heart pounded as I watched him slip along the ground. He wisely kept his eye on the furry form above him and paused each time the squirrel stopped scraping its teeth on the hard shell of the nut.

Finally I saw him stop, then slowly raise the shotgun skyward. As he lay in the prone position, he quietly pulled the hammer back and took aim. The distance of the shot, from where I sat, seemed to be about 30 yards. I wondered if the full choke pattern of the buckshot would find its target. I waited to see if Nathan would win the battle with his nerves.

Even when it's expected, a gun blast always makes me jump. When the report of the 20-gauge suddenly boomed in the big timber, I reacted with a startled jerk. I quickly recovered enough to see the gray squirrel fall sideways and plummet to the earth. Nathan looked back at me, and I gave him a firm thumbs-up signal accompanied by a smile that nearly broke my jaw. He sat up on his knees and reloaded. Then he stood up and carefully approached the downed prize. After making sure it wouldn't come to life and bury its teeth in his leg, he picked it up by the tail, turned my way, and held it high. I could see the beam on his face as he started toward me. There was a certain confidence in the way he deliberately crunched across the leaf-covered floor of the woods.

Later that evening the gray squirrel became one with us along with some fried potatoes, sliced tomatoes, and a big glass of sweet tea. (Excuse me while I drool!) The taste of success was delicious, thanks to Annie and her culinary talents. The day may have ended, but the memory of it will live on in my heart.

Since then there have been other things I have asked my son and my daughter to do that have stretched their comfort zones. As I have done so, I have tried to be careful not to challenge them if I felt they were not up to it. I was also mindful that they needed to start with small responsibilities before moving to greater ones. For example, when Heidi was young she was terrified by the simplest of things, such as going to the counter at a fast-food restaurant to ask for ketchup packets. For some reason, she resisted the chore until one day I asked, "Heidi, what are you afraid of? This is a prime opportunity for you to learn an important social skill. I believe you can overcome your fears and master your emotions."

While that little sermon might have been a little heavy for a seven year old, there was enough assurance from dad that soon getting ketchup packets was no problem for my daughter. As time went on she moved to weightier concerns. One of them was singing before an audience. Taking charge of her fear and dread of performance was eventually accomplished to the point that she now regularly sings with great confidence in front of auditoriums filled with people.

Of all I have ever set before my kids to do, I know the very hardest challenge they will face is to be in control of their moral behavior. I can only hope that the more manageable tasks, like sneaking up on bushytails or asking for ketchup packets, has provided a good foundation for their confidence. As they fight the fierce battle between good and evil, right and wrong, perhaps the simple "rehearsals" I was able to help them go through will benefit them.

In the same way that I made sure they were sufficiently equipped to do a task before I asked them to, God does the same for mankind, especially in the area of inner character. A vivid example of this truth is found in His words to Adam and Eve's son Cain. This young man was not happy that his offering was ignored by God, and he grew jealous of the attention that Abel, his brother, was getting for his sacrifice. God saw that Cain's attitude was less than acceptable so He presented him with an incredibly demanding task. Genesis 4:6,7 records God's words to Cain:

> Then the LORD said to Cain, "Why are you angry? And why has your countenance fallen? If you do well, will not your countenance be lifted up? And if you do not do well, sin is crouching at the door; and its desire is for you, but you must master it."

Question: Did God think Cain was able? Was Cain equipped to refuse jealousy? The answer is *yes!* Otherwise

God would not have demanded he do it. Did Cain respond positively? Unfortunately, no. Cain allowed evil to win, and his decision led to the murder of his brother. How incredibly tragic.

For those of us who live in this age of rapidly dwindling morality, we must ask ourselves, "Does God think we are equipped to rule over our flesh and all of its selfish desires, such as lust, greed, envy, malice, and jealousy?" The answer is found in 1 Corinthians 10:13: "No temptation has overtaken you but such as is common to man; and God is faithful, who will not allow you to be tempted beyond what you are able, but with the temptation will provide the way of escape also, so that you will be able to endure it."

Yes, we are *able!* If we weren't, we wouldn't be asked to be people of high standards. While self-control is an enormous challenge, it can be done. What do we need to help us rise to the task? What on earth can help us when we look heavenward and desperately ask, "Are you sure, God?" We need the same thing Nathan needed when he was deciding whether or not to go after that squirrel. We need what Heidi needed as she looked toward that busy counter at the burger shop. And we require the certitude I longed for as my mother handed me the guitar those many years ago. We need that divine nod of assurance our Father in heaven offers that tells us we can indeed face the battle for personal virtue...and win. We can do so with confidence because He thinks we are capable. And remember, in order to see that sacred, heavenly nod, we can look at God's words to Cain: "rule over it." The truth is clearly implied: *God thinks we're able!*

6

Nightmares

How could I ever forget that first morning of archery season when I overslept, rushed out of the house, and drove at land-speed records to win the race against sunrise. After quickly dressing at the truck, I literally ran to my treestand, climbed in and sat down on the small cloth seat. When I did, I felt the cold dew on the back of my legs that had fallen overnight. *Why is it so wet?* I asked myself. I dug through my shirt pocket and took out my flashlight. I flicked it on and couldn't believe what I discovered. I had forgotten to put on my camo pants! There I sat a quarter of a mile from my truck and all I had on my lower body was a pair of socks and shin-high rubber boots.

I couldn't believe it. With legs that were once considered by a major laundry detergent company to be used as the standard for white, I realized that every deer in the county would see me hovering over their heads like a fluorescent shop light. With so much skin exposed in the warm, early part of the season, I also knew I would be the gathering

spot for the entire mosquito community. Assuming the outcome of their attack might be fatal, I immediately considered returning to my pickup. But with the sun nearly ready
to light up the woods, I figured I could make it through the
prime hunting time, that first hour of daylight. I would not
be deterred.

I went ahead and pulled my bow up to my stand and
made another shocking discovery. In my scurry through the
brush, all but one of my arrows had fallen out of the quiver.
Once again I turned on the flashlight and checked the
ground below me. There they were. I could see the neon
green and white fletching in the leaves at the base of the
tree.

No way was I going to descend and retrieve the arrows.
I concluded that one deer was all I was allowed that day so
why would I need more than one shot? I nocked my lone
aluminum missile and went for my day pack to dig for my
release.

Oh no! Where is it? I asked myself in the darkness. I
searched my mental computer and there on the screen of
my confused mind was the data I didn't want to see. "Your
pack is still on the ground. You forgot to tie the shoulder
strap onto the pull-up string so you could hoist it up with
the bow, Dummy!"

Once again the flashlight came on. I thought to myself,
*If I have to turn this thing on one more time a ship is going to
dock here!* Searching the ground for the well-concealed,
camo-colored pack, I saw it at the side of the tree where I
had put my bow a few minutes earlier. I was in a pickle.

To say the very least, nothing was going right. I began to
think about all the other important things I might have left
behind and the other details I had probably overlooked as

I rushed to beat Mr. Sun to my stand at the edge of a corn-field.

Suddenly, as my head was chaotically spinning on my neck, something incredibly wonderful happened. I cannot tell you how grateful I am that it did. *I woke up!*

Hallelujah! It was only a dream. Blessed be! I almost got out of bed and did a dance of celebration, but I didn't want to wake Annie. In the stillness of the midnight hour, with my forehead slightly wet from sweating, I sighed deeply and smiled. The relief I felt was *almost* worth going through the trauma I had experienced. I drifted back to sleep to take advantage of the remaining two hours before the 4 A.M. alarm would sound to help me get to my stand on time that opening day of deer season. I did so with high hopes that I would have sweet dreams—not sweat dreams.

This type of nocturnal madness for a deer hunter might sound ridiculous to some. But when the first day of the season rolls around and you've invested countless hours in preparation and joyous anticipation of the event, it is not uncommon for a dedicated pursuer of the whitetail to experience the type of anxiety I did in my nightmare. I've talked to other hunters who have had the same thing happen to them in the middle of the night. They, too, always mention how happy they are that they woke up.

While most of us are more than elated that these dreaded dreams never come true, there are some who have actually lived one of these deer-hunting disasters in real life and, much to their surprise, the outcome was wonderful and successful. In fact, my friend Marty, who is basically a deer hunter by trade and has a part-time 40-hour-a-week job at the local post office, is a prime example.

Both of us live near the Kentucky border, and Marty has property there he can hunt. His work schedule dictated that he couldn't get across the border to set up stands until the first day of deer season. Bright and early he and his brother drove up and spent the day setting up their portables and tending to some food sources the deer would enjoy. They planned to return to the farm the next weekend when the cooler weather would stiffen the mosquitoes and activate the deer. When evening came, though exhausted and reeking with sweat, Marty decided to get into one of the stands and spend the rest of daylight simply observing a field nearby. With only smelly jeans, T-shirt, and no rubber boots to conceal his human trail into the woods, he climbed in and took a seat with bow in hand.

Not long after he sat down, Marty heard the sound that every deer hunter craves to hear. It was a crunch in the leaves behind him. With about 15 minutes of light left in that late September day, he slowly turned around and caught a glimpse of the biggest deer he had ever seen in his life. Wisely, he forced himself not to stare at the rack it carried. Words like "chandelier" and *"Pope & Young"* passed through his head and tempted him to sneak an extended peek at the antlers but he refused. Suddenly Marty found himself at full draw and, without pondering the situation too long, released an arrow. He heard that telltale thud that an aluminum, broadhead-tipped shaft makes when it connects with a deer.

As the buck kicked high and ran off into the heavy foliage, Marty made a mental note of the animal's escape route. With nature's light fading quickly, he descended the tree and stood at the base of it for a few moments. His thoughts were only of finding the "monster" that had made him suddenly wonder if he were dreaming.

Knowing Marty's hunting ethics, he would have been just as committed to finding a doe, but the once-in-a-lifetime prize that was bleeding somewhere nearby was intense motivation. He quickly gathered his equipment and his composure and met with with his brother who was surprised by the report. With their work commitments the next morning preventing them from returning to find the buck in the daylight, they knew they had a serious challenge ahead of them. After a quick cellphone call to the folks at home to alert them to what had happened, the two men headed for their truck, grabbed flashlights, and went back to the tree where Marty had drawn blood. They found the red-stained arrow right away and picked up a crimson trail within a few yards.

"I wish I could tell you that the story quickly ends," Marty said to me, "unfortunately this tale has some length to it." I was all ears.

The events that unfolded for Marty and his brother were indeed extensive. For the sake of time and space I offer a simplified version of his ordeal that lasted more than five grueling hours.

> Good blood trail. Blood on arrow along with smell of entrail contents. Gut shot! Churning in Marty's gut. Blood drops the size of a postage stamp. Drops reducing quickly to half-dime size. Hands and knees. Prayer. Two hours pass. Thirst unbelievable. Hunger worse. Mental snapshot of size of deer and antlers fuels search engine in Marty's mind. Creek bank. Fresh

tracks. Blood drop. Hopes up! Third hour passes. Deer spotted standing in creek. Still alive! Bolts and runs out of sight. Hopes down. Water in boots. Feels good on chest. Tempted to drink muddy creek water but thoughts of dysentery too troubling. Wait half an hour. Batteries dying in flashlight. Deer traveled at least one mile. Found again standing sickly on creek bank. Weaving. Unable to run (man...and beast as well). Must finish the kill. Sight pin hard to find in artificial light. Arrow released and buries in mud at deer's hooves. Second arrow nocked. "Thud!" Splash! Deer falls over eight-foot embankment into deep water. Floating. Two men barely alive. Deer dead. Long way home. Happy!

As I stood at the postal counter listening to his story, the patrons were stacking up behind me to hear the outcome. Fortunately, Marty was on a break and while others were able to get their business done, I was spellbound. Then, much to my surprise and delight, he reached behind the counter and pulled out the massive set of antlers and set them in front of me. Unbelievable! Twelve points to score for sure and four more that any deer hunter alive would count. The base of the rack was dripping with bubbled bone texture. The thing must've weighed five pounds.

Marty's story is proof that if you can live through them, sometimes nightmares that come true really do have good endings. And the fruit of enduring them can be very sweet. I discovered this to be true while standing on another type of platform much larger than that of my treestand. Annie and I took the concert stage one evening a few years ago for a radio station sponsored event. Thankfully the place was packed. We had arrived at the auditorium in plenty of time to get a sound check. Even though the sound system had some age on it, it seemed dependable enough. Little did we know that while we fed on our backstage meal, the system was feeding on itself. For some strange reason, it chose that evening to have an electrical coronary.

As the large room hummed with the sound of nearly a 1,000 voices, Annie and I waited offstage with our usual level of sobering respect for what we were about to do. Even after 25 years of doing concerts, we still get a little nervous as curtain time nears. I approach a concert in the same way I ride a motorcycle. I enjoy it but I never really relax. Each of us felt the kind of anxiety that is both good and disconcerting.

We heard the emcee say our names, and we entered stage left as the audience kindly welcomed us with applause. What took place in the next 90 seconds is hard to describe. To attempt to relate the full impact of what we lived through would be a difficult task. So in the same fashion that I condensed Marty's ordeal with his bruiser buck, I will try to tell you how the next 90 seconds of our lives felt like Marty's 5-plus hours nightmare. Keep in mind that if you've never faced 982 faces that have gathered expectantly to hear you perform your music, you might not get the full impact of this tragedy. Imagine, if you will, that you are in our shoes. Walk through this furnace with us.

"Good evening," I said into a dead microphone. Tap-tap with index finger on mike head. Nothing. Annie speaks into her mike. Sound level so loud ears in first row begin to bleed. Plug in guitar. Strum. Nothing in speakers. "Good evening." Silence. Strum. Dead. I step over to Annie's mike and quietly sing, "Mr. Soundman, lend me your ears!" I begged for mercy as well as audible levels on my mike and guitar. Nothing. Annie speaks again into her mike. Heard by family in West Virginia. Time slows to a mere crawl. Sweat forming on back of legs. Crowd very quiet now. Knees weaken. "Check...one...two..." Nothing. Strum. Audible only to me and 'Annie. Words of frustration begin to circle my mind like buzzards waiting for me to die. Won't be long. Temptation to let buzzards land denied. Seconds turn to hours.

Idea! "Annie, go get the live mike at the piano." She responds. I step to her mike and whisper to the bewildered audience, "Are we slaying you with our professionalism?" Kind laughter. Sympathetic looks. Annie removes mike from cradle and starts over to me with it. Cable catches on piano leg. Mike jumps out of her hand. Hits floor with a bang that rivals a nuclear explosion. Sleeping audience members awake. Some older ones grab left arms.

Strum. Guitar still dead. So are we. No one leaving. Must see outcome. Thoughts of murdering sound tech troubling but gratifying. Refuse to respond to instincts to kill. Smile nervously, reroute mike from piano and mount to my stand. Put guitar line in different channel in the connections off to my right. Return to live mike and say with a tired sigh, "Good evening!" Audience breaks into applause. Some believe it was all part of the act. We sing.

I honestly thought at one point that I was going to wake up and be so happy I was dreaming. It's terrible enough to be glad to awake from a bad dream. The only thing that might be worse is wishing you could go to sleep and stop dealing with reality. Nevertheless, we made it through the evening even though it undoubtedly remains the longest 90 seconds we have ever spent as musicians.

As bad as this catastrophe was, believe it or not, we found out a few weeks later that the evening had yielded a trophy that we were happy to lay at the feet of the Lord. As it turns out, in the audience that observed our bumfuzzled, chaotic, and unfortunately comical concert opener was a woman who presided as a judge. She was there as a guest of a family member and did not necessarily embrace the Christian frame of mind that we presented in our music. One of the songs we performed that night is entitled "Bring that Child to Me." The lyric expresses the cry of a barren woman as she appeals to an expectant mother who is planning to abort her child. The lyric begs,

> I am a barren woman
> I cannot have a child
> I've been a mother only in my dreams
> And the child you plan to throw away
> Could fill these empty arms
> Please let him live
> Then bring that child to me.[1]

We had no idea that the judge, at the time, was hearing a case regarding a matter that would decide for or against a local pro-life organization in the area. We were not only pleased to hear she ruled in their favor but that the song had moved her emotionally and the effect was life-changing. One other addition to the report was most gratifying and sobering as well. She told a concert staff person that because Annie and I had displayed such kind patience with the sound tech and auditorium personnel during our 90-second defaming in the beginning of the concert, she was much more open to the content of the presentation that, as it "just so happens," contained the song that touched a timely place in her heart. I shudder to think what damage might have been done had I responded to the urge to rant and rave that night.

Why is it true that what we would consider a personal nightmare sometimes results in a sweet dream-come-true for others? I once heard a preacher tell how a particular sermon he delivered, which he thought would be his ministerial masterpiece, came out like drool that dripped onto the pulpit and soaked his notes. He was so unhappy with his performance that he thought of dismissing the congregation in the middle of it, going home, skipping Sunday dinner, and spending the rest of the day licking his wounded ego. However, because he sincerely believed the truth that he longed for his people to hear, he verbally clawed his way to the end of the message. Then a week later, much to his amazement, he learned that the sermon he thought would get him fired was the very one that God used to persuade a soul to escape the flames of hell. Go figure!

I have concluded that it is during a living nightmare that we are more likely to depend less on ourselves and more on

God for deliverance. As a result, the "dreamer" becomes a visible example of the intervention of our unseen God. It was true for Annie and me with the concert we thought would never start. It was also true for the pastor who thought his sermon would never end.

For others of us, the bad dream that literally keeps us up at night is far more serious. A wayward child, a terminally ill friend or family member, the loss of a job, or the hurricane that looms off-shore, or whatever the case may be. The moment we find we are in the midst of a nightmare and turn away from self to seek the help of our mighty God, that is when those around us are most likely to be touched by His presence in our lives.

Perhaps you are in the midst of one of those perplexing dilemmas at this very hour. If so, please consider what drove my friend Marty to keep going into the night, crawling on his hands and knees and trudging through muddy creek beds as he tracked his prize buck. He had gotten a mere glimpse of the massive dimensions of the deer's body and rack...and that's all it took. In a similar way, may you now get a fresh sighting of the trophy of God's grace and the deliverance He has for you. If you do, it will help you find rest in Him until the nightmare is over.

> We count those blessed who endured. You have heard of the endurance of Job and have seen the outcome of the Lord's dealings, that the Lord is full of compassion and is merciful (James 5:11).

7

No Spikes

A couple of hunting seasons had gone by since Nathan had taken a whitetail. Though he had gone with me to South Dakota the previous year and harvested a huge mulie, his desire to outsmart an elusive, tasty, Tennessee deer was obviously eating at him.

Rifle season had arrived, and we headed to a friend's farm in the midstate region. Eddy, the property owner of the gorgeous 400 acres we were blessed to hunt, met us at his cabin on a Tuesday night. Another fine friend and hunter, Don, joined us for some food and fellowship.

As the four of us were finishing off our stew and eyeing the pecan pie that would soon find a place on the walls of our arteries, Eddy made an executive announcement. "No spikes! Let's let the young boys go on by this year." We all agreed, knowing that quality deer management was a wise decision. Plus there had been some good sightings of some mature bucks in the area. We then proceeded to la-la land

and dreamed of the big ones that would pass under our stands the next morning.

A few hours later we rendezvoused with daylight while sitting in our ladders, loc-ons, and climbers. Nathan usually chose the safety and comfort of the laddertype stand I had placed just off the edge of an alfalfa field. However, that morning he surprised me by picking one of Don's loc-on types. To understand my amazement at Nathan's choice you should understand one important item. When Don hangs a treestand, he has to get FAA clearance and mount red flashing lights to alert airplanes of its presence. Then he puts climbing steps on the tree trunk that requires a lover's embrace to make the ascent. And, along with a safety belt, a parachute is issued prior to the hunt. The best word to describe the feeling of the experience is "frightening." I could only surmise that Nathan was willing to risk life and limb because he knew that the placement of the stand was in an area that held incredible promise for an opportunity to fill his tag.

Around 10:30, the four of us regrouped at a place we call "The Dogwoods." We compared notes on the morning vigil. When Nathan gave his account of what had transpired for him, I found myself beaming with parental pride. I must confess that I was the proudest father who had ever lived and had a son. Why? Did he get a huge deer? No! He brought something out of the woods of much greater value.

He told us, "The sunrise was spectacular!" I thought to myself, *Yeah...and from the height you sat, my son, you probably saw it before the folks in Virginia Beach!*

"Everything was going great," he continued, "and about eight o'clock I was wiping granola bar crumbs off my mouth when I spotted movement on the logging road. I thought my heart was going to jump out of my jacket. It was all I could do to stay calm. I was so rattled that I had to stop and think about where the safety was on my rifle. The deer was coming my way. All of a sudden I saw it veer off the road and step into the brush, headed straight for my stand."

All the ears of us "seasoned hunters" were at full attention. I mentally made a note to thank Don for his expertise in stand sight choice. Eddy spoke up. "I didn't hear any shots this morning. What happened?"

Nathan looked at me, shook his head with a disappointed tilt, and finished the story.

"Well, Eddy, last night you told us what *not* to kill and, as it turns out, the only fur I saw this morning was on the back of a spike. He never knew I was in the world. He had some nice ones, probably five inches or more. But he was still a youngster. I let him walk. I must admit I did put him in the scope just for old time's sake. With the safety on, I must've pulled the trigger 100 times. It felt good to know he could've been mine."

Eddy's voice revealed the ache he felt in his heart for my young hunter as he thanked Nathan for the choice he had made. As I quietly struggled to keep my head from bursting my cap my mind went to Proverbs 10:1: "A wise son makes a father glad." The truth of the passage was suddenly fresh and sweet to my heart.

Following lunch and a power nap, we returned to the woods for the evening hunt. As I stood watch in my stand and listened to the music the cardinals and bluejays made, I pondered the choice my son had made that morning. As I did, I recalled an incident that had taken place a few short years earlier that required me to make a hard decision not unlike Nathan's. I was sobered by the thought that he was with me on that occasion. I thought to myself, *Could it be that the choice I had to make that day might have influenced the one Nathan had to make this morning?* I had a feeling it did.

Two or three years prior, when Nathan was around the age of 14, our family was at a church on a Sunday morning. We were to sing two songs as a "teaser" for the Sunday evening concert. We had completed sound check and were waiting in the pastor's office where we would meet him and his staff to pray together. All morning I had wrestled with the choice of the two songs we would present. Because our concerts have a theme (the family) and each song ties to the next for continuity, to sing only a couple of songs was comparable to the preacher delivering only 2 paragraphs out of his 15 pages of sermon notes. I was desperate to know what songs to choose.

Not long before the staff entered the room to pray with us, I finally settled on the titles and with a tone of confidence I made the announcement to the family. One was to feature the children. The other choice was accompanied by a distinct impression in my heart that the lyrics *should be* presented, as if they were prescribed medicine for a soul that would be present in the pews. I was very excited to have such clear direction. The song was to be "Father's Embrace." It deals with the issue of homosexuality and how a man's intense desire to know the love of his earthly father often contributes to a lifestyle that is not holy. Here is the lyric:

Father's Embrace

There are those who cannot understand
Why a man would take a man for a lover
And if you asked him why, he might tell you

"I was this way when formed in my mother."
But there are other words
Written in his life
Hidden in his heart
But seen in his eyes
His heart is crying,

"I need my father's embrace
I've tried other men's arms
But they cannot replace
The touch I have never known
I needed as a child
And now that I am grown
I still need
I need my father's embrace."

He was once that little boy who stood in line
Behind the other things his daddy held so dear
And he waited for his turn but it never came
Now he's a man with a heart full of little boy tears
But through the years no one has told him
There's a Father above
Holding out His arms
Reaching down with love
He hears him crying,

"I need my father's embrace
I've tried other men's arms
but they cannot replace
The touch I have never known
I needed as a child
but now that I am grown
I still need,
I need my father's embrace."[2]

Though convinced that this lyric needed to have a hearing in the morning service, I knew because of its touchy subject matter that I should clear it with the pastor. When the staff entered we greeted each other and prayed as a group. Just before the entourage exited I spoke up and informed the pastor of my lyrical intentions regarding "Father's Embrace." Without batting an eye or even a thoughtful hesitation, he firmly refused permission for us to sing the song and suggested we choose something more general in content.

As quickly as he came he exited, leaving our family standing there quietly stunned at his demand. After a moment of heavy silence, I said to Annie and the kids, "We'll do another song."

Nathan, our "red-headed intense one who likes to hunt" son, spoke up. *"Dad!* Are you gonna let that preacher keep you from doing what you feel God wants you to do?" The silence became even heavier.

With only a few minutes remaining before we would make our way to the spaces reserved for us on the front pew next to the pastor and his wife, my heart was swimming in turmoil. Nathan had asked a very legitimate question. I was instantly near the panic stage as I fought my instincts. Suddenly a thought came to me that had to have been divine. I'm convinced it was from above because of the fruit it bore in time. I looked at my seething son and then looked at Annie and Heidi who were also wondering what was going to happen.

"Family," I said, "we are here under authority, not in it. We must do what we're told and the results, whether good or bad, will be the responsibility of the staff. We will sing a different song."

Though my announcement didn't squelch Nathan's anger, we went about our business of why we were there that morning. Back at the hotel following lunch, I did not allow us to speculate on why the pastor so readily refused the song in question, although it was tempting to do so. We did express to one another the remorse for the one, or ones, whose lives might have been touched by the song. I then took the family to Matthew 8:5-10 to show them where I had heard the expression "under authority." The passage refers to the centurion who went to Jesus to ask him to heal his paralyzed servant who was suffering at his home. Jesus offered to go to the house and heal the man but the centurion said, "Lord, I am not worthy for You to come under my roof, but just say the word, and my servant will be healed. For I also am a man *under authority*, with soldiers under me; and I say to this one, 'Go!' and he goes, and to another, 'Come!' and he comes, and to my slave, 'Do this!' and he does it."

The centurion's understanding of how rank plays into the scheme of life caused Jesus to marvel at the soldier's faith. Luke's account of the story shows that upon returning to his house, the centurion found his servant had been healed.

I pointed out to Nathan that we did not hold the upper ranks at the church. We were there as underlings. To go against the authority of the church would have weakened what we were there to do.

Though it took some time, Nathan eventually accepted my decision to yield to the pastor. Since then he has had other opportunities to learn and relearn the important attitude of submission. In fact, he has mentioned to me on a few occasions how the example I was to him that Sunday morning has helped him avoid serious trouble with leaders in other situations that range from the classroom, to the workplace, to sponsors of concerts that he and his sister have done on their own. The most important aspect is that in his heart he has a respect for the highest of all authority—God.

Getting back to the evening stand that I occupied at Eddy's paradise… I sat looking in the direction of the big woods where Nathan sat high above the ground. I prayed for his hunt and his safety, and I thanked God for such a fine young man I could call my son.

I must tell you the hunt ended with all of us going home empty-handed. But for me, it was a red-letter day. No matter what the whitetail record books show, the most prized trophy deer in the world is the one that Nathan never killed.

8

It Takes One to Hunt One!

There is something about being called a turkey that falls somewhere between a humorous dig and a derogatory comment. For whatever reason, it never really offends. It just "hangs out there" and meets a need. The one who says it feels better, and the one who hears it is not left feeling devastated.

I'm not sure when or how it happened that the turkey became a laughingstock. To my knowledge, it never did anything harmful to anyone. In fact, there was a day when it was treated with much more respect. It is said that the wild turkey was Benjamin Franklin's historically famous choice for the bird that would be recognized as one of our national symbols. Why he chose it as a nominee or why it never received that place of honor would be interesting to know. I'm sure one could dive into the archives and find out, but why do that when it's a lot more fun to guess? (I know...I just lost the good graces of the history teachers, but hey, men rarely stop and ask for directions!)

Starting with the reasons for rejection, I can think of only two possibilities. One, it's just not the prettiest bird on the planet. With a face like that on our dollar bills and presidential emblems, it would be tough to look at them for very long and find patriotism welling up inside. Instead, we'd just sort of gag. The poor thing was not graced with handsomeness. The male, especially, got a serious whack in the kisser with the ugly stick. And to the die-hard lovers of the wild turkey, I'm sorry but that thing—that wattle—hanging off an old gobbler's face is really gross. I think they make medicine for that! I will admit though, from the neck down, it's a beautiful creature, which could be said of a lot of humans. (Don't look at me like that!)

Second, the flight of a wild turkey does not match that of the final choice, the Bald Eagle. There's something about the high-flying ability of the eagle that stirs in us a desire to rise above things such as ignorance and poverty. It moves us deep in our hearts. On the other hand, the soaring of a turkey is basically limited to getting in and out of bed, which could also be said of some people I know.

On occasion, the broad-breasted turkey must take to the air to escape danger, but they don't sail very far. Though pretty in flight as they leave the roost at daylight and whoosh overhead on their way to their kitchen table, they just can't get to the heights that an eagle can. Of course, if an eagle was packing enough food on its breast to feed a family of five, it too would have a hard time flapping its way into the stratosphere. The wings are there, the wind is waiting, but the "pot breast" of a turkey gets in the way. (This human resemblance to the wild turkey is getting a little too close to home!)

For whatever reason, you won't find the heavy, homely, and horrifically ugly face of a turkey on your silver dollar. Nor will it ever grace the banners that wave over this nation. The two birds in question have a lot to offer, but the bottom line is that *flying* was chosen over *food*. And that's fine with me.

Regarding the possible reasons that Benjamin Franklin presented the turkey as a good representative of America's positive traits, there are a few that seem logical. Could it be that the turkey was initially considered because of the food source it was to the people who lived here and for those who eventually settled on this continent? In my experience as a turkey hunter, there is a consistency about the breast meat that is both tender and tasty. As for the rest of the bird, I have given up on trying to nibble my way through the drumstick simply because the tendons and ligaments are akin to eating rubber bands and microphone wires. Forgive me, but I normally don't include that portion of the harvest in the cooking skillet. The domesticated, commercialized turkey does not seem to have this problem and it's likely true because they don't get the exercise a wild turkey gets in the forest.

Besides the food source, perhaps the wild turkey was looked at as our favorite fowl because it was plentiful. Their numbers, by ratio to the population, were far greater than today. Yet there seems to be plenty around in many regions for the modern hunter to pursue.

There were practical uses for certain parts of the bird. For example, those who fashioned their own arrows were more likely to use the feather of a turkey for fletching than any other type available. The length and strength of its quill and the width of the plume added to the arrow's durability and accuracy of flight. Furthermore, arrow making was more than the construction of a practical tool for hunting and self defense. It was a work of art. Because of that, turkey feathers were often used as vanes on the shaft since they held ample color and eye-catching marks. This was true then and remains so today.

Of all the reasons the wild turkey should have gotten the votes needed to occupy the office of "top bird," I can't help but wonder if Mr. Franklin's main reason for putting the *Meleagris gallopava* on the ballot was rooted in his love for hunting it. I have a feeling that after many frustrating attempts to harvest a turkey that ended in failure, he had developed a level of respect for the bird that was similar to the amount of esteem others gave to him as a leading citizen of the nation. It seems reasonable to believe that he had some exciting encounters with the incredibly effective eyesight of a turkey. And it's conceivable that he had discovered how nearly impossible it is to see a bird that stays on the ground through the daytime, feeding beneath the underbrush well below eye level of the average-sized man. As far as I'm concerned, if Franklin's feelings about the turkey were grounded in his sincere regard for its elusiveness, that alone is good enough for me. I say it's not too late to call for another vote. Yelp! Yelp! Hooray!

I admit there was a time when I didn't put turkey and deer hunting on the same line in terms of the excitement level involved. The reason was simple...I had never tried to bag a turkey. Then one day my friends Don Scurlock and Eddy Richey talked me into going along for a hunt during spring season in Tennessee. They warned me that I would never be the same after the attempt and offered me a chance to back out. I had noticed that when springtime arrived they were a little different than the rest of earth's inhabitants, and I'd often wondered why. But it was not until I yielded to their invitation that I would discover what made them look so wild-eyed and seem so skittish, especially during the months of April and May.

That first hunt was unforgettable. Don and Eddy instructed me that two things were extremely important. One, camo cover for every part of the body was absolutely necessary. Don even covered his eyes. And following his example, I shrouded my pump shotgun with camo tape. Without the proper concealment, there was no way to blend in with the surroundings and fool a turkey's highly sensitive peepers.

Second, they told me that when the bird is coming in, the slightest movement would likely spook it and send it scampering. The blink of an eye or a trigger finger sliding around to push the shotgun safety button had the potential to ruin the opportunity. I was cautioned that once a gobbler fixed on a hen call and decided to approach, my shooting position had to be already established, otherwise I would blow it.

There was enough exciting emotion in just the instructions Don and Eddy gave to cause my heart some considerable palpitations. I wasn't sure if the real thing would be survivable. Nevertheless, I ventured on with them to the fields that morning on my first turkey hunt. As we walked on the dirt road well before daylight, we kept our talking to a whisper. Don had "put the birds to bed," meaning he watched them from a distance the evening before and knew where they had flown to roost. Knowing they were overhead in the trees on a bluff nearby, we had to take care not to disturb their slumber.

In the darkness, Eddy put two decoys out in the field and then the three of us took our places along the treeline. Just after first light, Don began using a gift he possesses that is nothing less than remarkable. He had studied and practiced the wild turkey's language so well that he, with his man-made devices, could speak to them as if he were one of their own. (Imagine what Joy, his wife, would think about that compliment. And imagine what she's had to endure!) With a light, dainty clucking sound, Don broke the morning silence. His "waking up" call initially got no response. But he knew what he was doing. He waited a minute or two and with the flat, waterproof mouth call made of tape and latex rubber, he spoke again. Behind us, a bird responded. I froze. Eddy was motionless. Don slowly looked over at me and though I couldn't see his face behind the mesh camo mask, I could tell he was smiling. It was the way he held his head that told me his heart was racing faster than the pistons in a screaming Indy car.

Suddenly, I heard my very first sound of the swish of turkey wings in flight as a bird sailed off the bluff and glided down into the field. The grace of its soaring was impressive. So was its size. I didn't realize how tall a wild turkey stood. I wouldn't have noticed had I not been crouched low against a big oak. From where I was sitting, the eyes of the hen that had landed in the meadow appeared to be looking down at me. It was an awesome sight.

I was already in the shooting posture and had been there since we sat down. I took the instruction about minimizing my movement very seriously and was trying to be a good student. The problem that arose was excruciating, however. After about 20 minutes in one position, my body started to protest. My derriere had lost its feeling and the numbness was creeping up my back and was on its way to my brain. But to move would have spelled disaster. Although my arms wanted desperately to shake, I forced myself to hold steady and hoped relief would come quickly.

Finally a bearded bird descended into the field. The male is the only legal game allowed during the spring season and the sight of one was welcomed. As he landed near the hens, they briefly scattered. It was as if they were well aware that he came around only when he wanted "something." (Good grief! This man/turkey comparison thing is starting to hurt.) He had, indeed, shown up for the "ladies." Except for this special time in a gobbler's life, when "love" is all they are after, they usually stay away from the females and travel in bachelor groups.

Finding himself around several attractive hens, the male began his ritualistic strutting. With his tail at full fan, his head changed colors from pale gray to a brilliant red, along with some white and a hue of blue. It was a sight to behold. The problem for the three of us sitting there waiting for the chance to send him to turkey heaven was that he was too far away. Don was careful not to talk too much with his calls for fear of saying the wrong thing and causing the gobbler to run off. All we could do was sit by and hope he meandered over within range.

Suddenly things started falling into place. They were working their way around the field to where we sat. By then, the mixture of painful numbness and explosive excitement had started doing weird things to my entire body. I was an emotional and physical mess. Knowing I couldn't move, yet wanting to shake like I had grabbed hold of a live electric wire, I began to wish I had worn some plastic underpants. I was loving this new experience. In the stream of pure adrenaline that was rushing through my brain, I saw a reflection of the future. In it I could see all the seasons of springtimes yet to come, and I knew where I wanted to be when they arrived (if I was still around). I wanted to be at the edges of fields, tucked away in my camouflage among the leaves and branches, doing what I was doing at that very instant. Before I had ever pulled the trigger on one of these birds, I had become a bonafide, no-holds-barred turkey hunter. I had been "spurred."

As it turned out, none of us were able to score that morning. When the gobbler got within about 50 yards, he saw something he didn't like and scampered off to another part of the farm in search of companionship. The three of us gathered our decoys, seat pads, and wounded egos and tried another spot. Before 10 o'clock came I had managed to completely embarrass myself in front of one of the greatest turkey hunters alive. Don called in a huge, mature gobbler in another field, but I was much too anxious with my shot and missed the bird entirely. My friend was gracious and kept his ribbing to a minimum…at least until Eddy showed up. I have not been allowed to forget that blunder—and rightly so. I displayed the worse case of "feather fever" anyone has ever had. The bird should have been mine. It really is hard to draw a good bead when intense emotion makes my head spin around wildly on my neck! I hate it when it does that.

As an avid deer hunter, there's one thing I especially appreciate about turkey season. When the fall and early winter hunting seasons come to an end and the law demands that we deer hunters drop our weapons and surrender to things like our jobs and families, we start to experience withdrawals around late February. The index fingers of gun hunters, usually the one on the dominant hand, start to twitch and one eye closes involuntarily. (Bowhunter's twitches are far more profound and more embarrassing in public.) Then, when we face the disheartening reality that our legal return to the hunter's woods is several months away, we enter a certain type of depression. Talking intelligently becomes a chore unless, of course, someone asks about the deer we might have taken during the past season. We can be a pitiful sight around mid-to-late winter.

However, at about the time our loved ones are making arrangements to check us in at the local asylum for the depressed and troubled, something strangely wonderful happens. I warn you that it could occur at any given moment. For example, it might happen one day as you sit in your convalescent chair staring dejectedly at the linoleum. A caregiver walks into the room and asks, "Would you like a *turkey* sandwich for lunch?" Like an alarm clock, the word "turkey" rings a bell. Suddenly you lift your face and look toward the window. A bright light begins to shine on you, illuminating the entire room with an indescribable glow. Unexplainably, you stand up, raise your arms, and scream loudly, "Spring turkey season is only six weeks away!" Your family members get the call that you have recovered. You are back among those who embrace life as a wonderful thing. The doldrums are gone, spirits are renewed, and the smile returns to your face! That, my friend, is why turkey season is made for the deer hunter.

Don Scurlock would reverse my theory about the order of hunting seasons and the rehabilitative benefits they offer. He would say that deer season is therapy for the serious turkey hunter. And I fully understand his position now that I have had the privilege of joining him and Eddy in the gobbler game. In either case, we all profit emotionally by both seasons.

Some final observations about the wily old gobbler. I have to admit I have a lot in common with him. For one thing, that old bird might be ugly but he's smart. (Did I just insult myself?) And there's another thing that impresses me about him. It's in his nature to run at the very first sign of danger, and I have never seen one ignore that attitude. A mature male turkey is just that because he doesn't stay around for one extra second if he thinks his life or safety is in jeopardy. Like a wise old buck, he's out of there. I've arrowed a lot of deer because they stood there a moment too long after detecting trouble. I got the best of their curiosity. Not so for a woods-wise gobbler. He's gone at the first hint of trouble.

In the same way, in order to spiritually survive, I must understand that when an enemy (such as lust, for example) reveals itself in the area of my heart, if I don't flee immediately I get in real trouble. To hang around is a mistake. For instance, if I'm in a hotel room alone and far from home, I might be flipping through the TV channels. Suddenly I come upon a station that features smut. To momentarily pause and entertain a thought such as *I can handle this for a second or two* is a grave mistake. I know if I don't immediately turn the thing off or go to another channel, I run the risk of getting shot right in the eyes with a deadly round of eroticism. However, the smart move is to "flee [dart away like a turkey] from youthful lust" (2 Timothy 2:22).

I deeply admire the gobbler's attitude of willingness to forego the next grub worm, juicy bug, or even a fleeting, extra glance at the source of danger. He knows it's the key to his survival. I want to be like him. May I never forget that quickly running from the enemy of fleshly, unholy pleasure is the first step in avoiding the "flaming arrows of the evil one" (Ephesians 6:16).

With that worthy goal in mind, I will consider it a great compliment the next time spring season arrives in Tennessee and my sweet wife, Annie, looks at me in my boyish get-up of head-to-toe camo and facetiously says, as she often does, "Turkey—it takes one to hunt one!"

9

Wednesday's Prayer

Beyond the headlights of my pick-up I could see the bright glow of the well-lit truckstop convenience market in the distance. In the 4:30 A.M. darkness, the illumined sky above the store was like the welcomed beacon of a lighthouse. My morning drives to the treestand normally included an intermediate stop at this all-night mart, and this trip was no exception. As I let up on the accelerator and gave my right turn signal, my mouth began to water with the thought of the sausage and egg biscuit that had my name on it. When I mentally added a cup of coffee with cream and a packet of strawberry jam for the biscuit, I found myself dealing with some major saliva. On top of that, my knees grew weak with the thought of what awaited behind the glass in the case the store owners positioned right in the middle of the establishment. It was an original Krispy-Kreme Donut kept warm and soft with special lights inside the case. My insides nearly trembled with gastronomical excitement as I pulled into the lot, put the truck in park, and turned off the motor.

Already in the store were a couple of camo-clad gentlemen. One had his prehunt breakfast in one hand and hard-earned dollars in the other. The look on his face told me he had no doubt whatsoever that the investment he was about to make would be worth every cent. The other fellow was headed toward the coffee machine.

I was not dressed as they were. On my way to the woods I never wear my hunting clothes into a public place, especially one that reeks of overused grease, coffee brewing, and cigarette smoke. To a bowhunter, it's a serious no-no. It's bad enough to let the hair on my head (what's left of it) and my beard be exposed to such permeating odors, but with the use of a good face mask covered with an effective spray of scent neutralizer, the risk is minimal.

Though I was not readily identifiable as one of his own because of my "civilian" attire, I decided to strike up a conversation with the hunter at the coffeepot as he started to pour a cup of regular blend. I could tell he was anxious to get to the woods because of the gleam of anticipation in his eyes. It's the same countenance a kid has while waiting his turn to ride a roller coaster at an amusement park—an expression that a serious hunter would be hard pressed to hide.

"Well," I spoke up, "I hope the 'big guy' walks under you this morning!"

"If he does, I hope I don't suffer 'the big one.' My old heart might not be able to take it," he answered.

"Oh, I suspect you're ready for him."

As the man put a packet of sugar in his coffee, he replied, "I think maybe I am. I've been shootin' since June. My bow is tuned up and I'm pumped up! Got a great ridgeline to hunt, too. I hope the wind stays down today."

For the minute or so that followed, two strangers squeezed in more bonding time than many family members manage to accumulate over a week of Christmas visiting. I was loving it.

The gentleman closed the door of the donut case and as he headed to the clerk, I offered a parting word of encouragement, "Safe season to ya!"

"Thanks, man. Are you gonna get to hunt anytime soon?"

"I'm on my way right now."

He looked me up and down while trying to conceal the hint of doubt on his face that I was actually going to the woods and said, "Hope to see you at the checking station!"

I smiled and turned to grab the handle of the donut door. When I opened it the aroma of Krispy-Kreme made every taste bud in my mouth stand to attention. The smell carries with it many years of pastry perfection as well as a tradition of taste unmarred by the attempts of commercialism to change things until they are modern and unrecognizable. My hand almost shook as I reached in with one of those onion paper napkins to retrieve my prize. Since I allowed myself only one "cholesterol pill" per day, I quickly scanned the red plastic tray for the biggest one among the selections. I spotted one that seemed to be just slightly larger than all the rest and my hand was about two inches away from claiming my sweet treat. That's when it suddenly hit me. *It's Wednesday!*

Oh no! I groaned to myself.

With much reluctance I slowly drew my hand back, softly closed the glass door, and headed for the truck empty-handed. As I walked past the case that held the fluffy sausage and egg biscuits heated by flood lights, two of my senses (taste and smell) were in full protest. I unlocked the driver's door, climbed into the pick-up, and disappointedly started the engine. I backed out, dropped it into gear and pointed my low beams toward the farm 15 miles away. It was difficult and awkward to be on my way to the woods and not be steering the wheel with my right knee and stuffing my face with both hands. It just didn't feel right!

As the radiant brilliance of the truck-stop dimmed in my rearview mirror I began to regain my composure and was able to think clearly once again. I felt like I had just dodged a bullet. "How could I have nearly made such a terrible mistake?" I asked myself. "Perhaps it was the effect of too little sleep the night before." Whatever the reason, I almost blew it.

Why was I so troubled? Because Wednesday is the day of the week I have devoted to one of the most important activities I can ever do as a father. For years it has been the day I focus my prayers on my children, Nathan and Heidi. And even though it is not a comfortable thing to reveal due to the privacy required to do it correctly according to Scripture (see Matthew 6:16-18), I confess that I add a fast to the day. I do so in order to show the Lord how serious I am about my children's names being heard in heaven. That is the reason I would have felt terrible if I had been driving along cramming a donut into my face then suddenly realizing it was Wednesday.

From rising until the family gathers for the evening meal, I try to avoid intake of anything but water. As a result, at about midday when the old belly angrily growls for attention, I am intensely reminded to lift up my children to the Lord. To be honest, fasting is not always enjoyable, but the results are gratifying. It produces a great joy in knowing that my kids are covered in prayer. As the day goes on I strive to mention the needs Nathan and Heidi may have expressed as well as those I perceive they may have. There are also other parents with whom I have joined in praying for their children and, thankfully, they pray for mine.

In the solitude of the empty highway that led me to my treestand, I thought of my parents who provided the example of an unwavering devotion to prayers for their kids. Though P.J. and Lillian Chapman raised me right, there was a time when I chose the wrong way. In the early 70s I became a "spiritual mess" as a result of some ungodly decisions I had made, along with the error of keeping bad company. My folks suffered through those times, but not silently. They cried out to the Lord with their concerns for my spiritual state. In fact, they pounded often on the door of heaven.

How serious were they in their desire to see their only son committed to Christ? The following lyric reveals their fervency. In this particular case, it was my mother who worded a prayer over me when I was at the tender age of 13. Hers was a petition sent to heaven that rumbled the ground under this young buck. When I heard the words leave her lips, my blood ran cold that unforgettable morning in 1963. To help you understand why her prayer scared me the way it did, I must say that I had seen my mother pray and watched God answer her requests sometimes within a matter of minutes. As this lyrical story unfolds you'll see why it was on that day I first learned what "cold sweat" was all about!

Mama's Brave Prayer

One day in my early teenage years
Mama came into my room with tears
She said, "I've put it off too long

What I've gotta do seems wrong."
Next to my bed she fell on her knees
She laid her hard-working hands on me
Looked up to Jesus and told Him she cared
That's when I heard my mama's brave prayer.

"If you see he'll die a sinner
If you see he'll trade the right for the wrong
Then all I ask of you, sweet Jesus,
Go ahead, right now, and take him on home!"

She said, "Amen." And the room grew still
I'll not forget the fear I could feel
And the moments passed
So have the years
I'm glad to say that I'm still here.
Now looking back I can see it's true
She loved my flesh and my spirit, too.
Now heaven waits us and I believe I'll be there
And I'll be forever grateful
For my mama's brave prayer.[3]

The obvious question is why would my mother take such drastic measures in her prayers and risk the very life of her son? She did so for one good reason: She knew the worst thing that could ever happen to me was not that I wouldn't finish high school or that I wouldn't get a good job. Nor did she believe the worst thing for me was that I would marry the wrong person or someday be stricken with a deadly disease. As horrible as those calamities would be, she knew the most dreadful thing that could happen was that I would die without a relationship with the Savior. In her estimation, there was no other tragedy that could compare. It was for that reason she was willing to prayerfully "give me up" in such a way.

In 1974, after I passed through a season of spiritually wandering astray, the petitions she uttered years earlier were satisfied and I finally came home to Christ. My dad was in on the battle also with his weapon of prayer. How grateful I will eternally be that neither of them ceased in their cries to God on my behalf. I prefer to not even imagine where I would be had they given up. It is their example I follow in my prayers for my own children. What I want most for them has nothing to do with the temporal needs they may have. While I confess I would love to see them succeed in whatever they do with their lives, I long most that they know Christ and do His bidding. All else pales in the light of having a relationship with their Creator.

As I entered the gate of the farm I would hunt that morning and worked my way across the field to my tree-stand, I continued my battle with my appetite. Assured, however, that I was doing the right thing regarding the regimen of prayer I had established, I pulled my bow up to my stand and settled in for the hunt.

I had been conscious since four in the morning. When nine o'clock rolled around, my belly made an audible announcement that it was being rudely deprived of its portion of "daily bread"! The usual time this occurred was around noon. I knew it would be a long time till supper. As the clock slowly ticked the minutes away, I had to force my brain to reject the memory of the sausage biscuit and donut that haunted me. Wishing for the distraction that the flicker of a whitetail would provide, I scanned the woods for movement. That's when it came to me that I should redeem the quietness of the environment around my stand by mentally verbalizing some prayers for Nathan and Heidi.

I began listing the requests I consistently presented to the Lord on each Wednesday. "Give them peace and purpose, Father, peace through Christ and a purpose in His kingdom. Guide their feet and may your Word light their paths." Suddenly, as I repeated the plea I had voiced many times, the idea came to put the elements of my prayers into a song lyric. The thought that accompanied the notion was that there might be other parents who have yet to establish this kind of routine. Having a song they could hang their mental hat on might be helpful.

As I sat in my Grand Slam (an API Outdoors treestand, not a Denny's breakfast), I wrote the following words:

Wednesday's Prayer

Father God, to You I come
In the name of Your Son
I bring my children to Your throne
Father, hear my cry

Above all else, Lord, save their souls
Draw them near You, keep them close
Be the shield against their foes
Make them Yours, not mine

Give them peace in Christ alone
In their sorrow be their song
No other joy would last as long
Father, calm their fears

Guide their feet, Lord, light their paths
May their eyes on You be cast
Give their hands a Kingdom task,
A purpose for their years

And as my flesh cries out for bread
May I hunger, Lord, instead
That my children would be fed
On Your words of life

So, Father God, to You I come
In the name of Your Son
I bring my children to Your throne
Father, hear my cry[4]

If you are a parent who has yet to bless your children (and perhaps other kids) with a regular regimen of prayer, along with the discipline of fasting, I wholeheartedly encourage you to do so. And I'm glad to tell you that if you're a hunter, there is hardly a better place to spend time in prayer than quietly sitting on a deerstand, in a duck blind, or wherever your waiting occurs. It is a worthwhile way to redeem the time. Your stomach might not like you for it, but your children will be forever grateful.

> Devote yourselves to prayer, keeping alert in it with an attitude of thanksgiving (Colossians 4:2).

10

Borrowed Sorrow

One moment I was standing securely on the 20x28-inch treestand platform 18 feet above the ground. The next instant I was clawing for tree bark as I fell toward the earth. I vividly remember thinking as the stand let go beneath me, "Grab the tree!" As if in slow motion, yet as fast as a bullet, I watched the pattern of corky-textured bark zigzag by my eyes. I could almost see the tiny bugs in the crevices as I passed them on my way down. It was an odd feeling to be aware of so much so quickly.

I had been setting up an old portable-type climbing stand high in a forked tree with the intention of leaving it there permanently. It would hover over a very active trail that was used as a buck's scrape line the year before. It was well in advance of archery deer season and the mid-August weather was warm. I was in a T-shirt, cut-offs, and tennis shoes. Little did I know that as I was making my unplanned and rapid descent my arms, fingertips, and inner legs were being ripped to shreds. Somehow, though,

I didn't feel it. I did feel the sudden stop when the rigid, metal stand reached the forks of the tree about 4 feet off the ground. I folded up like an accordion and then fell over backward with my feet still in the straps of the platform. I was bent painfully into the shape of the letter "C" until one of the foot straps broke and left me dangling torturously by one leg.

I'm not sure how I did it, but I managed to get my other foot free. I plopped to the ground and groaned. With my life flashing before my watery eyes, I mentally assessed my whereabouts as well as the damage. When I realized I could feel my arms and legs, I rolled over and carefully stood up. I was dazed and embarrassed but grateful to be among the living.

Within a few seconds the feeling started returning to my fingertips, and they felt like they were on fire. As I wished I could put the tape in reverse and go back to the minute just before the fall, the insides of my arms announced their aching need for sympathy. Then the skin on my inner thighs just above the knees started pulsing with pain. Add to that the sweat that was seeping into the fresh open scrapes and cuts. I considered dancing to relieve the fiery sensations, but I was afraid something that was cracked might go ahead and break. Instead, I just started gingerly flailing my arms and walked around in circles like a chicken.

When I was satisfied that I was healthy enough to make it home, I did what any good man would do. I kicked the tree. As I nursed my toe, a horrifying thought hit me. "It's Thursday!" That's the day Annie and I normally do the last-minute preparations before leaving town for our concerts. "We travel tomorrow!" I mumbled as I reluctantly looked at the ends of my fingers. The small slabs of skin and meat that hung loosely on four out of five of the fingers on my left hand looked quite gross and hurt even worse. I didn't want to hear the answer to the question I asked myself: *How in this world am I going to play my guitar in just over 24 hours from now?* But I faced the hard facts. *The show must go on. I'll have to find a way!*

Then the reality of something even more awful came to me and nearly made me choke. Annie would have to see the mess I'd made of myself. That thought rivaled the physical pain of the hot-iron-on-the-skin feeling on my extremities. I knew Annie graciously tolerated the fact that hunting had its dangers. I was also aware she had heard the horror stories of treestand accidents that had left women either widows or perpetual caretakers of paralyzed loved ones. Now I had to go home and be living proof (at least I was living) that her dread was founded on truth.

With a grateful heart on being able to move, I faced the task of gathering my stuff with my wounded hands and heading home. As I exited the woods, the salty sweat continued to work its way into the "tree rash" on my skin. It felt like I was being raked with a wire brush.

Annie wasn't at home when I arrived. I hate to admit it, but I was very happy not to see her. I quickly washed and treated the abrasions and put on long pants and a long-sleeved shirt. The only things I couldn't conceal were my fingers. Unfortunately, I knew the Band-Aids on each of them would raise her eyebrows and generate the questions I didn't want to answer.

When she came through the back door my heart fluttered with dread. She looked at my hand and stared for a second.

"What on earth happened, Steve?"

"Oh, I had a little fall. I'll be fine."

Her expression told me she didn't buy the "little" part.

"And just where did this fall take place?" she asked.

At that moment I paused and thought to myself, *This would be a great time for the rapture!* I waited for the sound of a trumpet, but it didn't happen. So I answered, "Well...I did a little tree huggin' today."

My attempt at humor didn't bring a smile. She just stared at me. So I tried again.

"I rubbed a tree the wrong way this afternoon."

It was easy to tell when the truth of what had actually happened finally registered in her mind. The look on her face changed abruptly from an inquisitive squint of the eyes to jaw-dropping terror. I had hoped she would never have to ask the question that followed.

"You fell out of a tree?"

"Yes, ma'am," I responded with manly insecurity. I could sense my hunting days, at least from treestands, were probably numbered.

"And," she said as she looked me up and down, "I suppose the long-sleeved shirt is for a good reason."

"It ain't pretty under these sleeves," I said. I didn't even mention my legs. That would come at bedtime.

After showing my bubbling flesh to the woman who cared enough about me to show genuine sympathy for my injuries, we both went quietly about our chores. My first task was to uncase my 6-string guitar and see if the Band-Aids would allow me to depress the strings hard enough to get a clear sound out of them. Though it was quite painful, to say the least, I was able to get the tone close to the clarity I needed. I thought, *I'll just have to make sure we include some sad songs tomorrow night during the concert. They'll provide the best cover for the crying I plan on doing!*

There would be other repercussions to deal with as a result of "the fall." One came a few weeks later and surprised me. Little did I know that my lower back would have suffered an injury that would be permanent…at least it hasn't yet gone away. At times I make one wrong move and I feel like someone stabbed me in the posterior. It takes several days to recover, and it's terribly frustrating. The price my sciatic nerves have paid for an attempt at outsmarting a deer makes me look pretty dumb when I'm crawling from the bed to the bathroom. Or worse, when my wife is pushing me on luggage carts through airports. Thankfully, it's only an occasional handicap. Unfortunately, my crippling around only reminds Annie of how and when the injury took place.

Perhaps the most disturbing result of the fall was something I had to battle the very first night following the accident. Annie and I retired to bed and mutually avoided the subject of the fall. We talked a few minutes about other things then turned out the lights. As I lay there quietly staring into the darkness, I began imagining what *didn't* happen earlier that day. With no warning whatsoever, I found myself being tortured by the "what ifs."

What if: I was still hanging there because the stand lodged further up the tree? My feet would be broken and I'd be dead…or worse yet…still dying of suffocation. A search party would find me, grimace at the sight, and Annie would have to see it.

What if: I had broken my back, my neck, or both arms?

What if: I had been wearing the old waist-type safety belt? Would it have helped or, instead, squeezed the life out of me…slowly?

On and on the disconcerting possibilities invaded my night. Like soldiers of despair, they shot arrows of awful thoughts into my racing mind and heart. I was having terrible fits with my imagination. As the minutes passed, the tormenting "what ifs" only grew worse. For example, I could see the expressions on my parents' faces upon receiving the news that their son was dead or permanently maimed. I thought of the devastation Annie would face as a widow and single parent. Then I imagined the trauma of all the business chaos left to those I love, such as canceling concerts, endless legal settlements, and insurance claims. The menacing thoughts were tearing wildly through my head like a peace-consuming monster.

I was beginning to toss and sweat. My pillow became as hard as a rock, and I was filled with the fear of *all that might have been.* I assumed I would never get to sleep that night. Though my body was laying in bed, in my mind I was still falling out of the tree...and the bottom was nowhere in sight!

With my blood pressure elevating and my mouth as dry as desert sand, I was nearing the point of hyperventilation. Just as I was about to throw back the covers and head for a cold shower, a thought hit me that kept me from waking Annie and sharing my grinding ordeal. It was a truth I had heard years earlier, and it echoed in my mind with comforting repetition: *There is no grace for what* didn't *happen. There is no grace for what* didn't *happen.*

Those words began to drown out all other thoughts. As if someone were sliding a fader down on a mixing console used in controlling sound, the swirling noise of the "what ifs" that had risen to excruciating levels began to subside. They were gradually being replaced with reality as I coached myself with, "I'm O.K. It's only a few scrapes and bruises. I'm still breathing. Calm down. Don't borrow sorrow. There is no grace for what *didn't* happen."

The road back to inner calm was bumpy and curvy. Several times that night I had to regroup and resist the "what ifs." As I fought for peace, I wondered why it was such a difficult battle. Why would I have such a hard time getting a grip? The reasons are sobering. First of all, according to 1 Corinthians 15:22, because of the sin of one man, Adam, all humans are born with a sinful nature, with a propensity to fail. With that innate weakness in all of mankind, the enemy of our souls stands by "like a roaring lion, seeking someone to devour" (1 Peter 5:8). By allowing myself to succumb to the futile speculations and willfully entertaining that which *did not* occur, I had stepped out of the protective boundaries of security in the one who cares for me. (See Romans 1:21.) I began to lose trust in my heavenly Father. The result was that the predators of hell saw me helplessly trapped in the mire of my out-of-control imaginations, and they were moving in for the kill.

In my struggle to regain some semblance of dignity that night, I decided I had better make a fast move back to the real world. I began to make my mind dwell on better thoughts in the way that Philippians 4:6-9 instructs:

> Be anxious for nothing, but in everything by prayer and supplication with thanksgiving let your requests be made known to God. And the peace of God, which surpasses all comprehension, will guard your hearts and your minds in Christ Jesus. Finally, brethren, whatever is true [I was still alive], whatever is honorable [it was

good to go to God with my fears], whatever is right [don't give in to worry], whatever is pure [the love of God], whatever is lovely [Annie], whatever is of good repute [God is good!], if there is any excellence [I'll look for a better tree-stand] and if anything worthy of praise [I can still walk], dwell on these things. The things you have learned and received and heard and seen in me, practice these things, and the God of peace will be with you [peace was something I certainly needed].

I'm not quite sure how much longer I laid there in the stillness before rest finally came, but I think it was a good while. Each time the sting would pulse through my simmering skin I had to take my thoughts captive (see 2 Corinthians 10:5) and run back to His grace. With my heart rate at last back in the double digits, sleep came. I rested through the night and never woke to that battle again....

Then the alarm clock rang to alert us it was time to get ready to head to the airport. When I attempted to get out of bed, the fire that raged in my fingers, arms, and legs reminded me that I had to face the day with a resolve to keep my imagination in check. It wasn't easy.

I know I am not alone in my experience with the fall. I've met other deer hunters who have unexpectedly tumbled out of treestands. One fellow in Nebraska fell and was caught by his wedding ring on a part of his metal stand as he tried to grab hold of it to keep from going all the way to the ground. The weight of his entire body hung by one finger. That had to hurt!

The fact is...*it happens!* They say there are two types of treestand users: those who have fallen and those who have yet to fall. That's not a comforting or positive thought, but the impact of it can be motivation to strive for safer ascents and descents. For the sake of our loved ones, we who prefer elevated deer stands must do the right things such as letting them know where we are hunting and what time they can expect us to be home. Using an effective tethering device in order to prevent a deadly fall would also be helpful. It's not too much to ask.

One parting thought on the subject: For those who have been permanently disabled by such a tragedy or those who have lost a loved one as a result of this type of hunting accident, it is my prayer that you will know the comforting touch of God's peace and mercy in your hearts as you wrestle with the reality of grief. You would be the first to remind any of us who may be allowing the "what ifs" to whip us like a thug that there is freedom in the truth found in Matthew 6:34. I can almost hear you say: "Each day has enough trouble of its own. Don't waste your time and energy on borrowed sorrow. Save it for the real thing!"

> Let us draw near with confidence to the throne
> of grace, so that we may receive mercy and find
> grace to help in time of need (Hebrews 4:16).

11

Daddy's Shoes

I carefully attached my two-piece climbing stand to the tall, soft-bark tree and quietly ascended to a height of about 18 feet. Even with two inches of fresh snow on the harvested cornfield, I was confident it would host at least one whitetail out for its morning feeding. I settled in to enjoy the cold morning of hunting.

The end of the field I had chosen allowed me to observe the territory with the sun to my back. As it began to rise, so did my level of anticipation. Every moment was filled with excitement and hope, which is what makes deer hunting so attractive. There is never a dull moment, at least not for me. While others wouldn't care at all for waiting as motionless as possible for a whitetail sighting and might even find it boring, I cherish every second of the time I can be out in the woods. I've hunted long enough to know that no matter where I place a stand, even near a well-populated residential area, a deer can appear out of nowhere. Because of that, every turn of the head is filled with a potential prize for the eyes.

Perhaps the only other activity that can boast this type of nonstop, moment-by-moment potential is fishing. Each cast of the line teems with grand possibilities that the "big one" will accept the lure. Even when time is taken to change or replace the bait, the lull in the action is not dull to a serious angler. The line may be out of the water but the heart is still wet.

So it was that morning at the edge of the woods in my treestand. Every second was sweet, even while I dozed. After about an hour of basking in both the heat of the whitetail challenge and the warmth of the morning sun on my back, I saw movement in the distance. As is often the case, the activity was at the opposite end of the field. I could see a familiar shape working its way out of the high grass and into the openness of the 30 or more acres. The sunlight glistened on the shiny fur coat. It was too far away to tell if the deer was a boy or girl. I quickly retrieved my binoculars and focused in. It was a buck...and not a small one at that!

Through my glasses I could see the sun rays bouncing off the creamy, white-colored antlers. My trigger finger twitched as I watched the mature animal graze slowly toward the middle of the field.

Suddenly the creature was not alone. Another whitetail appeared. As I glassed the second deer, I could see it was more slender yet very similar in color. It followed the first deer across the openness and whenever the bigger of the two would look up, the smaller did the same.

About halfway between the three of us the field dipped into a small valley, just enough to conceal both of them as they turned and grazed my way. Then it occurred to me that because of the white oak acorns that nearly covered the ground below my stand there was a very good chance of getting a visit in the few minutes that followed. My heart rate escalated and my breathing became somewhat irregular. Somehow I remembered that I should be in the process of preparing for a shot so I slowly stood to my feet, attached my release and turned slightly sideways for a better angle at coming to full draw. Within 60 seconds I saw a deer's head bobbing side to side as it rose above the crest of the field in front of me. Atop the skull stood a sizable rack of antlers that certainly left me rattled.

As I coached myself to stand motionless and wait for the animal to get within range of my bow, I caught sight of something that caused me to quickly rethink my deadly plans for the lead buck. I got a good look at the second deer. He appeared awkward and innocent as he followed the older whitetail several steps behind. And standing straight up about four or five inches tall between his ears were the cutest set of pencil-sized antlers one could imagine.

For a reason that may be hard for some hunters to understand or accept, I began to feel certain about my hesitance to attempt a fatal blow to the older deer. I felt paralyzed by something I would not have done a few years earlier. I was "humanizing" the animals. To me they looked like a father and son on their way to a meeting of the local "rack-ateer's" club. I imagined that the boy had begged his daddy to let him tag along with him for the morning and dad had agreed. As they approached, I could almost hear the papa say, "Son, before we go any further we've gotta stop at that white oak just ahead. This year's acorn crop is some of the best I've had in my entire life. There might be a few left that we can find." And in the ear of my heart I could hear the youngster respond, "All right! I'm starving."

Before you yell "Bambi" in protest, let me admit I am very much aware of the danger of assigning human attributes to members of nonhuman realms such as plants and animals. Though it is not always intentional, too often it is used to misguide the very young and distort their perception of man's relationship with the rest of nature. As an example, as a child I had great difficulty with my uncles shooting and eating rabbits since "Bugs" was such a good Saturday morning friend.

Another illustration of an instance where undue human characteristics were applied to animals is found in the lady whose son and husband came home with the boy's harvest of a gray squirrel. The lad's sister saw the lifeless, limp body of the bushytail and showed great despair. The mother took full advantage of the girl's emotions, stooped to hug her daughter and began speaking with a tone in her voice that was utterly sad:

> Oh! I can almost see the mommy squirrel as she runs out on a limb in the darkness crying out, "Sammy! Oh, Sammy the Squirrel, where are you?" Sammy's sister is doing the same. "Sammy! Oh! Sammy come home!" Daddy squirrel is flipping his tail nervously as he calls out, "Oh! Sammy! Please come home!" And now can't you see his little family with their faces looking out of the hole in the tree, watching the woods, listening and hoping to hear the crunch in the leaves that will announce Sammy's arrival? But no...not tonight. Sammy. Poor Sammy the squirrel will not be going home.

Believe it or not, that mother was my sweet wife, Annie. I was shocked by her little story. As I wiped the tears...excuse me, as Heidi wiped the tears from her eyes she made me promise never to kill another squirrel. I conceded, and that was that. I'm just thankful she didn't do the same for deer.

While it is not always a good thing to wed human characteristics to nonhuman entities, one justification to do so is found in Jeremiah 17:7,8. In this passage a tree is actually granted human emotions to make an important point regarding the man who places his full confidence in the Lord.

> Blessed is the man who trusts in the Lord
> And whose trust is the Lord.
> For he will be like a tree planted by the water,
> That extends its roots by a stream
> And will not fear when the heat comes;
> But its leaves will be green,
> And it will not be anxious in a year of drought
> Nor cease to yield fruit.

A tree is said to neither have fear nor to be anxious. While we know that trees are incapable of such emotions, the implication is that when our trust is in God, we have the greatest source of life and comfort. It is ours in the same way a tree thrives by growing alongside the life-giving bounty of an active stream. Still, in this biblical case, a nonhuman thing was assigned feelings reserved only for mankind.

As the two bucks fed like hungry lumberjacks on the acorns beneath my treestand, I was amazed at how easy it was to not put the bigger one in my peep sight. Believe it or not, even though I have shed the blood of many deer in my day, occasionally something such as this happens that touches a soft spot in my heart and makes me act out of the ordinary. So it was that morning. Though I wasn't sure exactly why, the pair beneath my stand simply made me melt with melancholy. There was something about them that struck a chord deep in my soul. I just couldn't take the shot.

Before too long they both apparently had satisfied their appetites and wandered off into the timber behind me. As the sounds of their steps in the frozen, crunchy leaves were fading I decided to call it a day and come back another time when I would be in a less pensive state of mind.

Prior to heading to the truck, I took the opportunity to examine the two sets of prints in the snow. It would be a good chance to gain a little insight regarding their size and weight. I walked out into the cornfield to the place I had seen them appear on my side of the little valley and began to follow their tracks toward my stand location. I carefully observed the depth and width of each set of prints. Then I noticed something most intriguing. For several yards the tracks of the youngster were right on top of those of the older deer. As though he intended to do it, the adolescent was matching the adult step by step as they walked through the snow.

When I saw the two sets of tracks stacked together, I was suddenly very happy I had let the well-antlered buck (and his offspring) go on by. I was pleased because the two of them reminded me of another father and son. While standing in the expanse of a cornfield in middle Tennessee, I was swept back through time to a town in southern West Virginia. There I saw my dad and me walking through a white blanket of snow. It was 1955, and my father was on his way to Sunday morning church. Behind him, in my red rubber boots, I struggled to keep the wet powder out of my shoes as I followed. Then I discovered that if I stepped into his tracks I could keep the frigid snow from finding my little feet. So even though it was a struggle to reach his footprints, I stretched my short legs as far as they could go and managed to let my boots fall down into the wide imprint he stamped into the snow. It worked. When I got to church, my socks were quite dry. When service was over and we walked back home, I was careful to do exactly the same thing.

As I left the cornfield that morning and made my way back to the truck, I was filled with the joy of knowing I had been fortunate enough to have had a father who provided a good set of bootprints to follow through time. Looking back at the tracks he left for me through the years, I know they led me to knowing Christ, the best of all destinations. Also Dad's steps have guided me to a belief that things like a good name, honesty, and integrity are far more valuable than gold or silver. And I'm confident that if I continue to put my feet where my dad puts his, the tracks will lead me to heaven.

When I climbed into the cab of my pickup and started the motor, I sat staring out at the field I had exited. As I did, the lyrics to the following song started forming in my head. During the drive home, I wrote them down.

Daddy's Shoes

Daddy's shoes made a deep impression
In that West Virginia snow
I put my feet where he was steppin'

He left a real good trail to follow
And he led me home that winter day
Back in 1955
That was years ago but I can say
That in this heart of mine

I'm still steppin' in the tracks
Of my daddy's shoes
It's a trail I love to follow
Cause it'll lead me through
And when life turns cold and bitter
I'll just do what I saw him do
I'll make it safely home someday
Steppin' in the tracks of my daddy's shoes.[5]

sc

When I arrived home I parked the truck, walked to the patio, and proceeded to stomp the snow off my shoes. As I did, something caught my eye. It was my son's rubber boots sitting by the back door. For a long moment, I remembered the tracks in the cornfield. I thought of my dad and I thought of my children. I prayed, "Lord, if they follow in my tracks, may they lead to You!"

The steps of a man are established by the LORD (Psalm 37:23).

12

Crosses on Highways

As a traveling musician, I have spent untold hours driving on America's highways. Leaving town to sing in a faraway city has a certain excitement about it. However, the happiness usually wanes about 50 miles down the road. There's a vast difference between *going* there and *getting* there. The latter is by far my favorite part.

While traveling full time can be a chore like any other job, there are some discoveries along the way that make the journey interesting. For example, Annie and I were on an interstate in Tennessee and drove under an overpass. On one of the concrete support columns I saw two words written with blue spray paint. They read: "Trust Jesus."

I said, "Annie, look. Its 'evandalism!'" She chuckled and returned to her book as she shook her head in amazement.

Another spray painted message caught our attention in Florida. On the side of a bridge there were large red letters that read: "Jimmy loves Mary." Then with black spray paint, there was a line through the first statement and a newer message written to the right. It said: "Not no more!" We couldn't help but wonder what had happened in that relationship.

Then there are the bumper stickers that provide some lighthearted moments. My favorite is: "I'm low on estrogen, and I have a gun!" And how could we forget the septic tank truck that had this sign printed on the back: "We Haul Milk on Weekends."

Annie loves to ride and read. She can go for hundreds of miles with her face in a book...as a passenger, of course. Not me. I can't read for very long before I get the urge to do some cookie tossing. Fortunately there is a wonderful activity I enjoy, and it's one that fits very well into my blaze-orange psyche. I highway-hunt the great whitetail deer. Before the wardens call for directions to my house, let me quickly say that this does *not* mean I pull off the road and take shots at wild game from the cab of my vehicle. Nor does it mean I deliberately used my van as a "Chevy.06" and go after "grilled" venison. It simply means I am constantly scanning field edges and wooded hillsides for the sight of deer. It has become a habit I suspect will never be broken. For an avid hunter, it sure makes long trips more tolerable.

Two warnings though: Even though this pastime can be incredibly exciting, highway-hunting can get a fellow in a heap of trouble if he's not careful. And it usually happens when his wife is beside him and the two are rolling by a meadow of healthy alfalfa in rural America about 30 minutes before sunset. Out of nowhere she says something like, "Honey, did you ever ask anyone to marry you before you met me?" He looks in her direction but focuses on the field beyond her. Suddenly he says excitedly, "There's one...no...

two…five…no wait…there's at least eight! And they're nice ones, too!" Things get really messy when this happens.

Second, a hunter of the highways is not always safe to ride with. Annie has been known to request that she become my designated driver. She'll tell you the signs that reveal a hunter's intoxication with deer sightings. Some of them are:

1. staring for more than 30 seconds out of the driver's side window at a 50 acre, freshly cut cornfield while doing 65 MPH

2. twitching index finger

3. sudden removal of hands from the steering wheel followed by an uncontrollable full-draw motion

These signals will alert any wife or other passenger to the imminent danger he or she faces. Demanding to trade places with an overstimulated highway-hunter is the only safe thing to do!

There are other things that occupy our attention "on the road." One particular practice that Annie and I have noticed along the roads in increasing numbers through the years causes our emotions to swing from the jovial to the sobering. When we pass the objects placed there, we are invariably moved to contemplate their meaning. We see them along interstates and highways, as well as on street corners in towns all across our land. They appear in various sizes, and each one is uniquely decorated from the simple to the elaborate. They are crosses placed at locations where a loved one or a friend has encountered an "appointment."

These places have become sacred ground to folks who are left to deal the best they can with tragedy. While state and local governments may own the property, in the hearts of the grieving the real estate belongs to them. No one alive can take away the connection they will forever feel to that place on the highway.

I am impressed with the concessions given to the presence of the crosses by those who are in charge of clearing our roads of debris. I have yet to see one taken away and discarded. Such consideration for others who have invested the time to perpetuate the remembrance of their loved ones in such a way is a great act of kindness. It is also a vivid indication that they, too, know the reverence signified by the memorials.

On the way to a farm where I often hunt, there are three small crosses at an intersection. They have been there for at least two years. The report I've gleaned from the locals is that a high school senior was giving two girls a ride to their home. His speed and inexperience resulted in the loss of control, and the three young people instantly passed from this life to the next. The depth of love for the teenagers is represented by the three wooden reminders that stand just off the edge of the road. There are names written on each one, and they are adorned with colorful, plastic flowers.

From time to time, I noticed one or two of the small structures blown over by the wind from passing vehicles or perhaps a strong weather system. On more than one occasion I have parked my truck and placed the crosses back into standing positions. To be honest, I feel a slight connection to these families. I don't know their names, and they don't know about the care I've given to their memorials. Yet I do so because their efforts to bring to the living a visual reminder of the existence of the three youths moves me in my very soul. I would want someone to do the same for me.

After tending to the crosses one afternoon, I journeyed on to my treestand and took my seat. As the evening sun followed its daily path to the horizon, I couldn't get my mind off the painted wooden forms I had briefly held in my hands that afternoon. I realized that in some garage or workshop somewhere nearby a dad or brother, perhaps a sister, mom, grandparent, or friend also once held the pieces of pine. I imagined that with tears he or she sawed the wood, applied the white paint, and carefully tapped the small nails that held them together. The gripping emotions that tore at the heart as he or she lovingly wrote the names of the children on the dried white paint must have been deeply painful. Then, with some type of ceremony the "carpenter" and friends gathered at the place along the road and hammered the crosses into the ground. The rain had long since washed away the salty tears that dropped into the grass as they stood for a while and remembered the youthful faces that would not be seen again until eternity. I whispered a prayer for the unknown friends I now have. I wished them well.

Then an idea came. I decided to do my part in adding to their attempt to ensure that their loved ones would not be forgotten. I would build my memorial to them in the best way I knew how. I would write a song about the act of love that they and many others have displayed on roadsides in the form of crosses. It would not be written to refresh their sadness. Instead, it would serve to assist those of us who are untouched by their grief to not overlook the memory they hold so dear.

Abandoning my grip on my bow, I took my pen and started the lyrics that follow. I sincerely hope the next time you are traveling and catch a fleeting glimpse of a cross on the side of the highway, you will pause in your heart for just a moment and embrace the sight. May it stir a prayer in you for those represented by it.

Crosses on Highways

Crosses on highways
Handwritten names
Places on earth
Where the angels came
To walk through valleys
So deep and wide
To carry souls
To the other side

Old and young
But all too soon
Empty hearts next to
Empty rooms
Words too deep
So hard to say
But spoken well
By crosses on highways

"We will miss you
Till we see you again
We will kiss you
On your picture
Now and then."

Crosses on highways
Handwritten names
Places on earth
Where the angels came.[6]

13

He Did His Part

Every hunter who uses a compound bow understands the forgiving mechanical phenomena that occurs when nearing full draw. It is the point at which the bow "breaks over" and the poundage suddenly drops anywhere from 65 to 80 percent, depending on the brand and set-up of the equipment. It allows the hunter or target shooter the luxury of being able to hold at full draw with much more ease and, thus, a longer period of time. It's extremely helpful when, for example, an unsuspecting deer walks into bow range and stops behind a tree. When it halts, the only thing showing is its head. Instead of letting the string down and alerting the deer's highly sensitive eyes to the motion, the hunter can continue holding at full draw and hope the animal takes a few more steps, presenting the vitals as a target.

With traditional archery, the bow does not allow such a reduction in pull weight. As a result, the shot must be more fluid and quickly completed. (I deeply admire the traditional archery hunters. They are a special people!) Not too many of us could keep a 65-pound recurve or longbow at full draw for very long before starting to shake uncontrollably. However, a compound set at the same weight with 80 percent let off could potentially be held back through the entire hunting season. (A stretch, of course, but you get the point!)

As user-friendly as the break-over point on a compound is, there is a condition that accompanies a hunt that can still make it nearly impossible to get to full draw, something familiar to us all. It is called buck fever. As a victim of this debilitating, momentary disease found only in hunters who are overstimulated by the sight of deer, I am personally acquainted with its perplexing effects. Whenever I spot the shape or color of a whitetail anywhere near my stand, a switch is tripped in my brain that makes my muscles tense up like I'm having a total body charley horse. Oddly enough, the condition worsens as the deer moves closer. Any of us who hunt the whitetail will admit it can be frustrating to deal with buck fever. Yet it is that level of excitement that constitutes the very reason most of us accept the challenge and keep going back to the woods year after year.

Holding a gun steady for a good, clean shot while fighting the merciless effects of this illness is hard enough. An even greater feat is trying to smoothly pull back the string of a bow when conscious rigor mortis has set in. The one thing that can help a rattled hunter overcome this problem is to develop the muscles by lifting weights, doing push-ups, and getting into good physical shape. But even with that having been done, there was a time when I found that the "moment of truth" nearly made a liar out of me. It was during my first elk archery hunt in Montana with my friend and expert elkster, Randy Petrich.

Long before the September for my hunt came, I had met with Randy when he and his wife came to a concert Annie and I did in Nebraska. While we visited, I asked him a question that started the ball rolling toward a painful next few months for me. I inquired, "Randy, what poundage should I be shooting when I come?" In the back of my mind I knew what a comparatively low weight I shot and that his answer would not be what I wanted to hear.

"Steve," he replied kindly, "you ought to be shooting at least in the 60s. Preferably mid-sixties. A 'pass-through' shot would ensure quick death, and if we have to track him, it'll help with a good blood trail."

I quietly nodded my head as if to indicate I was already at that range of weight. However, Randy must've seen the nervous twitch that immediately attacked my face because he asked, "What weight are you shooting now?"

I desperately didn't want to answer. I knew very well that my response might give him a coronary, then I'd be out an outfitter. But because I believe there is no softer pillow than a conscience that is clear, I gave him a truthful answer. I said, "Just under 55 pounds. I'm not really strong in my upper body, but I've taken a lot of whitetails at that weight."

Randy looked down for a long moment. (Either he was checking out the shine on his shoes or he was praying for wisdom to know how to put into words what he was about to say.) With a courtesy that was most appreciated, Randy posed a question, "Well, Steve, is there any way you can move your draw weight up about ten pounds?"

At that request, I felt my shoulder joints explode. Even the thought of getting the string back on a bow in the mid-sixties range made me squeamish. I'm aware that lots of men do it all the time, but I'm not one of them. The Lord gave me Barney Fife-styled biceps, and that's what I have to work with. And it's been fine for me in Tennessee. However, the idea of going to Montana with greater muscle mass in my upper arms and back was about as remote a possibility as winning the Mr. Universe contest.

With absolutely no confidence that I could do it, I offered Randy the very best false hope anyone could deliver. "Sure. I'll try to move it up to the mid-sixties. I'll be ready."

"That'll be good. If you'll do your part, I'll do mine." he responded.

His parting words rang in my ears for days. They scared me. To do my part would require much more depth of commitment than I had known in terms of physical conditioning. I went home from Nebraska that April and faced my dilemma the way any grown man would do it...I cried. Well, not really...but it might have helped. As I looked ahead to my September journey to the west, I imagined the moment a huge bull might stand broadside near me. Just the speculation of it made me weak in the arms. I realized I was headed for the hunt of a lifetime, and it was conceivable that I might not be able to close the deal. But sometime during early spring I made the decision to upgrade my strength to a level that would handle at least 63 pounds of pull weight. I asked myself, "Can I do it?" I thought about it for a while and said to myself, "I've gotta try to do my part!"

Cardiovascular endurance was not the problem. I had already been on a regimen of a three-mile run on an every-other-day basis. Well, running is not what I do, it's more like jogging. Well, not really. Its actually a fast hobble, although using the word "fast" is overstated. Let me put it honestly. It's a spry but tentative motion. Nonetheless, I manage to make it three miles round trip on a consistent basis. I was confident that my legs were in pretty good shape.

On the other hand, my upper body was in need of serious attention. My plan was to start with 5 push-ups in 4 repetitions during my 3-mile hobble. That would be a total of 20. I would do that for the first two weeks and later start adding to that number. I did just that and by mid-summer I was doing 80 push-ups each time I went hobbling.

All through the summer I was also gradually increasing my bow weight until finally by early August I was consistently drawing around 64 pounds. I was quite pleased with the accomplishment and couldn't wait to tell Randy about it.

Moving ahead to September 23, 5:45 P.M., on a mountainside in the wilderness of the Gallatin National Forest in Montana....The test for my new level of strength was pending. We heard a bull bugle on the mountain above and to the right of us as my friend Eddy and I sat atop our horses on a forested flat about a mile from camp. Randy bugled back and when he did, another bull answered below and to the left of us. We were caught in the middle. As Eddy and I followed Randy's excited but quiet signal to dismount, he also said, "Grab your bows and let's head downhill. The wind is in our faces and that bull's a little closer. He sounds like a nice one!"

As we approached him, the elk bugled again, but this time only about 100 yards away. I had never been that close to an angry bull and the monstrous voice with which he spoke literally made the hair on my neck stand straight out. It was an ominous sound that shook me to my very core and mercilessly introduced me to "bull fever," which is best described as buck fever on steroids.

When we were just a few yards from stopping to set up for the final attempt to entice the bull within range, the wind suddenly shifted. The evening thermals began to drift over our backs and blow directly toward our target. Randy was concerned and softly said, "Let's sit down right here and hope the wind changes again. Otherwise, he's gonna smell us and we'll never see him."

As we knelt in the soft, pine-needle-covered soil, we waited and quietly talked about the situation we were in. As Randy was looking downhill, his eyes suddenly got bigger than fried goose eggs. Excitedly he whispered, "Steve, nock an arrow. The bull's coming in!" I was kneeling in the prayer position and I quickly took an arrow out of my quiver, loaded up, and attached my release to the string. As I was beginning to change positions in order to accommodate my right-handed shot, Randy begged, "Don't move. Just get ready to shoot!"

There I was, facing straight ahead on my knees, and a heavily antlered elk was running full blast toward us. Instinctively, I slowly raised my bow and then called on the five months of vigorous exercise I had done to do its job. As the bull came within 60 yards I attempted full draw. Much to my surprise, however, I got nowhere with the string. It felt like I was trying to pry apart the steel bars of a jail cell. I couldn't believe it.

The bow shook violently as I tried to overcome those 64 pounds and when it did, the arrow jumped off the rest. It fell alongside the riser but amazingly did not detach from the string. As fluidly and rapidly as I could, I replaced the arrow on the pronged rest and once again attempted full draw. I'm not sure if I had lost torque by being on my knees or looking straight ahead or both. But for some reason, it required something akin to labor pains to even start the string to come back. My arms shook, my body shook, the mountain shook, the horses trembled, Randy and Eddy shook, all of God's children shook.

From somewhere deep within me, a determination rose up that demanded I not be defeated. By then the bull was within 45 yards of us and still coming in. Resolved to give it my best effort or break my arms trying, I continued battling with physics. Then something wonderful happened. I'll never forget it. I reached the break-over point of the bow! It was such a satisfying feeling. When the limbs, pulleys, cable, and string slipped into that position I was as relieved as if I had just given birth to a baby. (I'm sure all moms would take issue with my comparison!) But really, I felt an ease in my arms that was as welcome as the first day of archery/deer season in Tennessee. It seemed that the summer filled with 320 or so miles of hobbling and over 5000 push-ups had paid off!

I found out later from Randy that as he sat next to me watching the bull with one eye and me with the other, he had never seen anyone show such composure and determination. I took his statement as a compliment even though I was unbelievably embarrassed. He also said something that was soberly interesting. He noted that when I got to the break-over point in my draw I let out an audible, heaving grunt as the poundage quickly reduced to a manageable level. He said that when I did, the bull stopped dead in its tracks. He must've heard me and halted to check out the sound. It was that loud!

When the bull did stop, I put him in my peep sight. As it turned out, his head was behind the left trunk of a forked tree and his rump behind the right fork. In the middle was his lung area, the very target I needed. The problem was the tree separated only about 14 inches and was 20 yards away. A thousand calculations went through my spinning brain and I came up with the guess that by the time the arrow got to the forks of the tree it should have ceased any slight fishtailing action a shaft might do when it is released. I made the assumption that the shot would look like the hundreds, if not thousands, of others I had made over the summer, and find its way between the trunks. I judged the distance at 35 yards, put the pin on him, and put careful pressure on the release trigger.

I can still see the orange fletching as it sailed between the forks of the tree and plunged into the side of the bull. He kicked and ran. From Eddy's vantage point, he saw that the fletching was barely protruding as the animal ran off. That meant even though it wasn't a pass-through, the arrow had penetrated well.

Years of dreaming and months of preparing culminated into a few momentary seconds of time. I nearly collapsed from the adrenaline that had saturated my system. I was glad I was already in the praying position.

After finding a small pool of blood, a brief search allowed us to spot the elk in the distance below our position. With his binoculars, Randy carefully examined the wounded animal and determined the hit was good enough to be fatal. We waited about two hours into the darkness, started another search, and jumped the bull. Randy wisely decided we'd all return to camp and continue the pursuit the next morning. To say the very least, it was a long night for me.

Daylight found us back at the spot we last saw the elk. Within just a few minutes, Eddy found the blood trail and the next minute Randy glassed the hillside below and saw the bull laying below us at about 75 yards. The joy we shared was unforgettable.

If I had a dollar for each time I've replayed that shot in my mind, I could buy the Gallatin National Forest. Every time I recall it, I feel a tidal wave of gratitude wash over my soul. I'm extremely thankful to have been able to be in such a pristine place and to take on the challenge of pursuing the majestic elk. Add to that the gladness of being able to bring home the delicious evidence of the hunt! From my teen years filled with looking at *Outdoor Life* magazines and dreaming of an elk hunt, to that April when I felt the pavement under my palms during those first five push-ups, to watching the orange plastic veins fly between the forks of that tree, I will cherish each element of it separately and collectively.

Perhaps one of the most gratifying memories of the entire adventure is found in Randy's challenge that was made months before: "You do your part, and I'll do mine!" He definitely came through as a guide. And, thankfully, though the shot did not come easy, I was able to rise to the occasion. I shiver to think what might have happened had I not sufficiently prepared. Randy would have skillfully enticed the bull into my range, and I would've been left with memories of an unsuccessful attempt to get past the break-over spot on my bow. Not only would it have been terribly disappointing, but the outcome would have made

Randy's effort a waste of a lot of valuable time (not to mention Annie's and my hard-earned dollars!).

Sometime after the elk meat had been tucked away into our freezer and the 5x5 rack had been hung under the patio to season, Annie and I were at the home of some friends. I was retelling the story of the hunt. (Yes—they asked for it!) As I was boasting of my conquest, I came to Randy's "you do your part and I'll do mine" section of the tale. At that point Annie chimed in and reminded me of something our son experienced a few years earlier while in junior high school. It had a hauntingly familiar ring to it.

When Nathan was in the eighth grade, he came home one day with a very poor math test score. He plopped down on the couch and mumbled something about how God didn't hear and answer his prayer about an exam he had taken that day. Annie asked him what kind of mark he had received on the test, and he replied, "Fifty! Where was God?"

Annie's next question revealed something that resulted in one of the best lessons Nathan ever learned:

"Did you study for this test?"

Nathan's answer was honest. "I studied a little, but mostly I just prayed and asked God to help me pass it!"

The wisdom our son received from his mother that day forever changed him.

"Nathan, it sounds like God did His part. You just failed to do yours. Think about it. If you would have put forth the effort and studied, your poorest grade, lets say a 49, would have resulted in an A. Don't expect God to allow you to avoid responsibility. He wouldn't be a good heavenly Father if He did all the work. Next time, just make sure you do your part, and He'll do His." With a motherly pat on

Nathan's arm, Annie added, "And by the way, there's one more thing you must not forget. When you pray for God's help for the next test and you study and pass it, be very careful to give Him thanks for doing His part...and for helping you do yours. Otherwise, you may say in your heart, 'my power and the strength of my hand made me this [grade].'"

To say the least, I was humbled that evening by the recollection of Nathan's encounter and his mother's wise admonition. As a result, I was able to see an important picture in my elk story. Just as Randy kept his promise as a guide, God never fails to come through with His side of the bargain. The question is: Do I hold up my end of the deal? And when it is done, do I give Him thanks for helping me do it?

May all of us remember that whether we've struggled to the successful side of the break-over point on our compounds or we stand back and look at what might have been accomplished in other parts of our lives, we must be careful to give the credit for the higher percentage of the final grade to the one who deserves it.

May God be praised for helping me in Montana. He definitely did His part!

14

When I Walk These Fields

After maneuvering my climbing treestand to a height of 18 feet, I pulled my bow up with a thin line of rope and began the process of settling in for the morning hunt. With only 20 minutes of darkness remaining before the light began to fill the woods, I quietly attached the straps of my mechanical release around my wrist. As I did, I suddenly felt an emotion that I knew better than to suppress. To do so would have been a grave mistake. It was a feeling I would compare to a fever that alerts the body that something is wrong. (To put it in biblical terms, it was like the godly sorrow that leads to repentance (see 2 Corinthians 7:10).) The feeling that engulfed me was *guilt*. And it nagged at me in the blackness of the forest. Its purpose was to motivate me to make an important decision.

What was causing such a disturbing emotion? There's no other way to explain it than just to answer honestly. The hunt I was trying to enjoy was one of too many absences from home I had racked up that fall. The Tennessee archery season runs from late September to the end of October and sometimes to early or mid-November. That's around 45 days. By the time I had ascended the tree where I was sitting, I had gone to the woods on at least half that number of mornings. That was admittedly a lot of predawn soundings of the alarm clock. Those wake-up calls not only woke me, but they also brought a night's rest to an abrupt end for my wife, Annie. My exit from the comfort of our warm bed also meant that she had to hear me fumble around in the darkness of the room as I dressed and tried to move to the door without turning on a light.

I assumed it didn't phase her. She rarely, if ever, stirred or groaned to indicate it did. Little did I know (until I asked) that many times after I closed the back door our dog, Bob, that sleeps on the floor beside our bed, would decide he needed to go outside and mark his territory again. Consequently, I didn't know that several times as I pulled out of the driveway thinking I had successfully departed without annoying anyone, Annie was on her way through the kitchen to open the door for Bob. The worst part of it was that once Annie awakes it is nearly impossible for her to go back to sleep.

So there I sat in the wonderful quietness of the presunrise hillside staring out into the woods. Soon the calm forest would reveal its beautiful shapes and glorious autumn colors as the coal-black night submitted to the welcomed sun. Wanting to take it all in without distraction, I was sorely tempted to ignore the feelings of regret for having added one more "X" to the boxes on the October calendar that revealed my overindulgence in hunting the great whitetail.

I began to argue with myself. One side of me said, "Don't you know you deserve to be out here, Bubba? You work hard, my man!"

The other side replied, "Maybe so, but can't you get too much of a good thing?"

"But the meat! Good source of nutrition for the fam. Gotta fill the freezer, you know."

"Yeah, right! For what you've invested in deer meat you could buy a grocery store franchise. Who are you trying to kid?"

"Hey! I need this solitude. It's good for the soul. Besides," and it was inevitable that the *ultimate* excuse would be presented about that time, "this is a great place to commune with the Creator, right here in the middle of what He's made!"

The sensible side was silenced for a moment. It always happens when the "spiritual benefits" defense is used. However, the motive behind that argument was not hidden to the light of truth.

"You always try the fellowship-with-God-is-good-out-here tactic. You ought to know better than that by now. Why don't you just admit it? You're obsessed with this huntin' thing! You eat it, sleep it, and drink it. When three o'clock comes and you can't go back to your treestand for the evening you fidget like a second grader that has to go to the bathroom. And it irritates you when you get up before daylight and have to go to work instead of going to the woods. The only thing that consoles you is if there's a heavy downpour and you know the huntin' wouldn't be so great anyway. C'mon, Chapman. Face it. You're a sick man!"

That side of me was making way too much sense. I tried the righteous and pitiful defense. I was sure a little self-esteem and a little cry for sympathy would get him off my back. "Look! I'm a decent fellow. I don't barhop and spend money on worldly and immoral stuff. Why beat me up? I just need a little R&R occasionally. Being out here is a way to open the pressure valve and relieve the tension. I'm always a better man to be around after I've spent time in the woods. It's good therapy."

Once again, for a brief moment, the side of me that represented good judgment was silent…but only for a few seconds. Suddenly, without warning, the argument came that would render my self-centered ego completely speechless. It had happened before, but not for a long while. It caught me totally off-guard.

"Let's get back to Annie. She's the wife of your youth, your dove, your undefiled one, the woman you made promises to in the presence of God and witnesses. Several years ago you told her you would cherish her and devote yourself to her every need. What happened, Bubba? Do you really think she's not affected by the bells that consistently go off on your nightstand at 4:30 in the morning? Are you naïve enough to believe she doesn't notice that when you leave you don't at least gently kiss her on the cheek and say a quiet goodbye? And you rarely let her know exactly where you'll be hunting. Do you think she doesn't worry about you? Do you think she never imagines that you might be lying lifeless under one of these trees when it's well after dark and you haven't shown up?"

For the first time all morning the conversation was conspicuously one-sided.

"And furthermore, what makes you think for one minute that Annie doesn't see that faraway look in your eyes when she's trying to talk to you sometimes at night. While she is sharing the deepest feelings in her heart, you're messing around in your head with two things. One, where to set up a stand to rendezvous with that buck you've been chasing.

And two, how you're gonna break the news to her that you'd like to go huntin' again the next morning…instead of going to town with her!"

The initial onset of guilt felt that morning was a mere pinprick in my heart. It would have been manageable. However, by the time Good Judgment finished his speech, the remorse I was feeling had left a wound in my heart big enough to drive my pickup through.

Funny thing was…I was right! I had not been the man I had promised Annie I would be. In the same way that the darkness of the morning was giving way to sunrise, it was painfully dawning on me that when autumn comes I can be practically worthless as a husband. Annie truly was one of those "deer widows" people joke about. Suddenly it wasn't humorous. I was guilty of abandoning her from September until the law prohibited me to enter the woods with a weapon in late November or December. Yes, I might have shown up physically at home, but mentally I was in the wilderness.

I sat there in my climber completely stunned by what I was feeling. There were two very distinct sensations welling up in my inner being. The first was an intense shame for having been so oblivious to Annie's feelings regarding the way my hunting might have been affecting her…and us. Sometimes my blindness was admittedly intentional. At other times it wasn't. Either way, it wasn't good.

The second emotion that came was an incredible flood of gratitude for the woman who I assumed was, at that very moment, wide awake and brewing a pot of coffee that she would share…alone…again. As I imagined Annie sitting there by herself with only Bob as company (and he was probably asleep—males are all alike!), I started feeling like pond scum.

With the top half of the sun now splattering the hillside with hues of yellow and red, my heart overflowed with a fresh love and appreciation for my sweetheart. I could hardly contain the thankfulness I felt for what she meant to me.

Then something really strange started happening inside my head, and it was most unsettling. A tear was actually trying to break through the rusty old gate of a duct in the corner of my eye. To be honest, it surprised me. It had been quite a while since love had done that to me. But I couldn't stop the flow. The mixture of love, good guilt, and gratitude was forming as a salty liquid, and it ran down my cheeks making it hard to focus on the beauty of the morning woods.

As I took in the sight of dawn's first light, I was struck by a comparison. I thought, *Annie is as faithful to me as the sun that greets this continent every morning. It is devoted to warming our lives and brightening our way. That's what Annie does for me!*

In the next moment an idea came to me that required some action: *I'll write a poem to Annie.* Knowing it would be a display of gratitude worth pursuing, I dug in my camo pants pocket for the pen and paper I always take with me to the stand. With my bow resting on the railing of my climber, I was poised to document my love for my wife. As I scanned the woods for any movement among the trees, I waited for the right words to come. These are the first words that made it to paper:

> When I see the sunrise I think of you
> How you're faithful and true to me.
> When I hear the bluebird's morning refrain
> I hear your name...so lovely.

"Whoa!" I excitedly whispered to myself. "She's gonna love this and kiss me all over!" Unfortunately, as quickly as the inspiration had come, it seemed to disappear. As the minutes passed I felt stuck between a heart full of feelings and a pen that wouldn't move. *Where do I go from here with this sonnet?* I desperately asked myself. Then I reread the lines I had scribbled on the paper and realized I had just used my surroundings as a backdrop for the word picture I was attempting to draw. That's when I started looking around for other comparisons.

> Sunny skies, your eyes.
> Sweet smell of the pine
> Brings you to my mind.

I felt like I was on a roll but I knew the next line had to be a good one. It needed to be the part of the poem I would go back to when all else was said, like the chorus of a song. I decided to not only consider where I was sitting in Tennessee as a source for that special image, but I also started recalling as many places I had been around the nation as I could. I searched my memory for that scene that had left me breathless. That's what I wanted for the next line.

As I mentally hovered over a map of America, I was drawn to a spot in the state of Texas. It was there, in a huge field near the home of our friends Charlie and Carolyn Norman, that I found what I was looking for. Earlier that year I had stood there and beheld perhaps one of the most glorious sights in the universe...a field of Texas blue bonnets in the spring. My pen began to move.

> When I walk these fields where the bonnets are blue
> It's a lovely view...and I think of you.

After about 45 minutes of enjoying the task of searching the great outdoors for just the right examples of sights and sounds that could compare to my beloved Annie, I had myself a poem. Here it is in full:

When I Walk These Fields

When I see the sunrise I think of you
How you're faithful and true to me
When I hear the bluebird's morning refrain
I hear your name so lovely

Sunny skies, your eyes
Sweet smell of the pine brings you to my mind
And when I walk these fields where the bonnets are blue
It's a lovely view...and I think of you

When I see the ivy that grows on the vine
I think of the time you grew on me
When I see the young fawns in the meadow at play
I think of the way I am with you

Sunny skies, your eyes
A warm April wind
Your touch on my skin
And when I walk these fields where the bonnets are blue
It's a lovely view...and I think of you

Sunny skies...your eyes
The dance of the stars
Your love in my heart
And when I walk these fields where the bonnets are blue
It's a lovely view...and I think of you[7]

About an hour had passed when I carefully folded the paper and slipped it into my shirt pocket. I knew I had to—

no, I actually I wanted to—dismount the treestand right then and return to the house with my offering of handwritten love. The prospect of seeing Annie smile when I read the poem to her drove me to go. The ripping sound of separating velcro echoed through the hollow when I removed my release. The noisy clatter of metal on tree bark further broke the silence. But I didn't care. I was so determined to communicate my feelings to Annie that it wouldn't have mattered if a *Pope & Young* class buck would have appeared. I was not going to stay.

When I pulled into the driveway earlier than usual, I was sure Annie would assume the crunch of the gravel meant it was her cue to get the camera, come outside, brag on another deer, and go on and on about what a man her man was. It was a pleasure to think how surprised she would be to find that, instead, I was coming home early just to have coffee and talk to her. However, I was disappointed to discover she was not there. I found out later she had an eight o'clock hair appointment in town 25 miles away.

In the quiet of the house another idea came to me that overrode the temptation to hurry back to the stand. "Get the guitar and turn this poem into a song!" Within an hour, I was ready to sing my way into the husband hall of fame. My heart pounded with excitement at the thought of doing what I had planned. When Annie came in I would take my guitar, sort of like Ricky Nelson might have done, and serenade her with a musical rendition of the words I had scrawled on the wrinkly paper.

Sure enough, when she came home around 11 o'clock and sat through my apologies and my melodic attempt to rewoo her with my caterwauling, she reacted just the way I had hoped. She wept. (I hoped it didn't sound that bad.) As she got up from the table and walked toward the Kleenex box on the counter by the phone, I felt a little bad that I had caused her to cry. Well, not that bad. I was honestly pleased that I had managed to connect with her. She commented on how sweet it was that I thought of the things I had written and thanked me for the word picture I had drawn of my love for her and what she meant to me. At that moment, she smiled then pulled out one of our favorite lines from the Andy Griffith show. It was from the scene where Brisco Darling is responding to Aunt Bee's reading of a poem. Annie lowered her voice as if to mock Mr. Darling and said in a southern drawl, "It was your heart...speakin' to my heart." Enough was said. She had paid me the highest compliment I could get!

Since that morning we have talked openly about my obsession with "the other deer." (It's spelled two ways, you know). I was careful to tell her that I recognized her restraint in scolding me about it. Her response was intriguing to say the least—and sobering as well.

"Steve, I'm not your mother. I'm your wife. It's always better when you can come to these conclusions on your own. We're both better off that way. I know if I nag you about something it only leads to conflict and a power struggle. Instead, I just pray for you. I have to trust God that He'll work on your heart. I also have to trust that you're mature enough to want His will. If I didn't detect that in your heart I'm not sure I could do as well. But, hey, look what He's done this morning...and I'm grateful. I'm just delighted that you responded to His call the way you did."

At that point my blood chilled at the thought of what would *not* have been happening just then had I pushed away that first tinge of guilt that had pricked me earlier that morning.

As the day went on I reflected on the kindness Annie had shown me through the years. I realized her attitude about not wanting to mother me had been in place all along. I thought of the time about ten years before when I was training for a marathon. The only word of advice she offered throughout the months of daily long runs that took me away for hours at a time was, "Those knees are meant to last a lifetime, Steve." Other than that she let me run myself right into the operating room at our local hospital. Three months after the December completion of the 26.1 mile race in 1990, I had knee surgery. There is permanent injury to prove she was right. Yet she didn't do the "I-told-you-so" thing. She knew I would admit my error—and I did. The good news is she loves me anyway.

Where had I gone wrong with my love for the great outdoors in terms of my relationship with Annie? Basically, I failed to follow the instructions for husbands found in 1 Peter 3:7: "You husbands in the same way, live with your wives in an understanding way." If I had chosen to understand her feelings about how much I was disappearing in the fall of the year I would not have been dealing with the guilt and regret of my actions. Instead, I had focused on me and the whitetail. Its not easy to admit, but I was dead wrong to do such a thing to my wife.

Further into our discussion about the untold number of days I had not been there for her during deer season, Annie noted that she was not the only deer widow in America. She had seen the looks on women's faces after concerts that told her they too struggle with absentee husbands. I started trying to recognize those expressions as time went on and sure enough, I saw them, too.

As fellow hunters come to me after concerts and we swap stories of our whitetail exploits I see a gleam in their eyes. However, very often right behind them are wives that stare into the distance and sometimes at the floor. Often they just walk away toward the lobby. Recently one lady confided in Annie and me about her struggle with deer-widowhood. She said, "I do O.K. with his hunting…until about mid-season. That's when I start feeling pretty lonely." Unfortunately, that sentiment is all too common among wives of hunters. Their complaints are legitimate.

When that tender woman shared her deepest feelings with us, I silently prayed for her and all the wives who carry the same burden for their marriages. I asked the Lord to hear her cries for help and, in the meantime, to trouble the hearts of husbands who over-hunt just as He had done for me. I prayed for the men who were so caught up in the challenge of outsmarting the eyes and ears of a whitetail that they could neither see nor hear the cries of the women who were forgotten and who were afraid their husbands were out of control.

Fellows, I appeal to us all. Turn your peep sights toward home. There you'll find greater trophies. Don't refuse to understand your wife and what pleases her. And let me urge you to do something that can make a real difference in your relationship with your wives: Next time you are in the woods, or going there, and you get that sudden jab of guilt that alerts you to your own struggle with "buckaholism," don't ignore it. If you do, you'll regret it.

If, by chance, you are reading this confession of mine in your treestand and you sense the urge to do something special for your wife, why not write her a poem? If you don't think you can do it, feel free to use "When I Walk These Fields," as a pattern. Or you're more than welcome to use the poem as is. However you do it, be sure to verbalize the feelings of your love and appreciation for your mate. I know from experience it'll get you some points as a husband. And, after all, to those of us who love to hunt the whitetail, "points" really matter!

Now, gentlemen, let's *"buck* up and *doe* the right thing!"

15

"Where's Dad?"

As an avid, passionate hunter who feels the temperature of the breeze of time slowly dropping, bringing with it my winter years, I consciously embrace every opportunity to go to the woods. Though it's not as easy to climb the hills and ascend into the trees as it used to be, I still get that anxious longing to be out there.

To say that I am a middle-aged hunter would be a stretch. If that were so, I will live to be a hundred. According to the averages, I passed the midlife mark at age 35, a depressing thought for those in their thirties. I am also well past "the big 4-0." Someone once said that 40 is the old age of youth and the youth of old age. How true! Now that I am significantly beyond that point, I've noticed some changes in my body that are common to all who are in the late autumn of life. This condition, brought on by the passage of too many years, is vividly described in chapter 12 of the book of Ecclesiastes:

> Remember also your Creator in the days of your youth, before the evil days [old age] come and

the years draw near when you will say, "I have no delight in them"; before the sun and the light, the moon and the stars are darkened, and clouds return after the rain [the despair of aging]; in the day that the watchmen of the house tremble, and mighty men stoop [bent over with age], the grinding ones [teeth] stand idle because they are few, and those who look through windows grow dim [the eyes]; and the doors [ears] on the street are shut as the sound of the grinding mill is low, and one will arise at the sound of the bird [old folks get up with the chickens], and all the daughters of song will sing softly [let the early risers not be suddenly disturbed]. Furthermore, men are afraid of a high place and of terrors on the road [bravery wavers]; the almond tree blossoms [white hair], the grasshopper [private parts (excuse me)] drags himself along, and the caperberry [an aphrodisiac] is ineffective [say no more!].

That pretty much sums it up for me. Well, not yet, really. But in order to brace myself for the inevitable fact that the day will come when my heart wants to go hunting but my body won't cooperate, I am doing one thing that might spare me from the depression that often grips the aged. I am carefully protecting my memories. I am placing them in a scrapbook found on the shelf of my brain. Knowing that someday when I'm unable to (or not allowed to) go hunting, I'll at least have my collection of mental hunting videos to replay and enjoy.

That's what a man named James probably assumed, too. He was robbed. At the ripe age of 74, something sinister began to steal from his mental scrapbook full of snapshots taken while sitting on his deerstands. It plucked from his mind the sound of the laughter once shared with his hunting buddies. It slowly took away each recollection of the nervous thrill that accompanied the sight of a whitetail cautiously walking into a field. Gone were the echoes of the gun blasts that followed the careful squeeze of the trigger on his Winchester rifle.

James fought hard against the beast that feeds on precious memories, and it seemed that he had totally lost the battle. It appeared that he had completely given up. Until one day, somewhere in a room in his mind, he must've found one small picture that had fallen from his scrapbook and was left behind by "the thief." His discovery resulted in a response that shocked those around him who loved and cared for him. The following is an adaptation of the story of James told to me by a friend during a drive to a hunt in Tennessee.

———•———

Phillip wiped his feet on the mat in his garage and stepped into the kitchen. He had been outside searching for one particular person. Not finding him outdoors, he hoped to locate him as he scanned the faces of all those who had gathered for Thanksgiving dinner. After checking the rest of the house, he realized there was a missing family member. He walked back into the kitchen area, drew in a deep breath, and with a dread for the commotion his question would undoubtedly cause, he forced himself to raise the volume of his voice and ask it.

"Where's Dad?"

For a long three seconds a hush fell over the room and everyone looked around at each other. Suddenly the crowd of adult siblings, teenage grandchildren, and one invited boyfriend disbursed. As if they knew exactly which direction to run, the group immediately became a well-organized search party.

The object of their search was James. The elderly father of four was last seen sitting in his favorite chair quietly staring, as usual, at the sound-muted football game on TV and enduring the noise that had filled the house.

With a year of catching up to do, Phillip and his brother and two sisters had been talking rapidly as they worked together to put the final touches on the dinner. It was during that information-packed conversation that Phillip, the oldest of the four, looked through the dining room into the den and saw the empty chair. He excused himself to find his dad. His first thoughts were that his father was destroying the bathroom again with his "bad aim." Not finding him there, that's when his quest began.

James was a victim of Alzheimer's Disease. Initially his children thought their dad's altered behavior was a result of the intense grief he felt over the loss of his wife of 51 years just two winters before. As the months wore on, the episodes of memory lapses grew worse until they finally coaxed him into seeing a doctor. Upon learning about the ongoing debilitating nature of the condition their dad would experience, each of the children mutually agreed that they would be his primary caregivers. With Phillip's house as the base, they all pitched in and did their parts to the best of their abilities.

Even with the quality of the care their dad was receiving from his offspring, there were still a few times that James had disappeared, causing a great uproar. Fortunately, he had never wandered far—once to the storage shed where he was found sitting on the Snapper lawn mower and another time he was discovered in a neighbor's pickup truck.

Fifteen minutes had passed and no one had been successful in the search for James. Allen, the youngest, stood with one hand on his hip and the other on his forehead and spoke with a tone of voice that revealed his desperation. "Where is dad? How could so many of us let him just vanish?"

Martha, the oldest daughter, suggested, "Let's comb the neighborhood. He's gotta be around here somewhere."

The rural setting boasted of only four homes lined up on the north side of the highway, sitting about 200 yards apart. After a few minutes the crowd regrouped on the front lawn and reported no success. Anna, the youngest daughter, suddenly noticed that Phillip's Chevy S-10 truck was missing.

"Phil! Where's your little truck? Did you sell it?"

The panic on her brother's face was much too obvious. When he turned to run into the house to get his Blazer keys, the entire family went with him. They knew something awful was unfolding.

As Phillip ran through the kitchen on his way to the garage, he glanced into the laundry room. What he saw stopped him dead in his tracks. There in the middle of the linoleum floor were his dad's house slippers.

"What?" he mumbled anxiously to himself. "Where's...?"

He stopped mid-question when he noticed his hunting boots were gone. Then he saw the empty hanger hook where he kept his camo overalls.

"Oh no!" came the cry of a son whose heart was racing. "Dad's gone hunting!"

Just then, Phillip's wife joined him in the doorway of the laundry room. "Phil, do you think your dad has headed to the woods?"

"I hope not, Honey," he answered, "but you know how much he used to love going out. And yesterday was the first day of gun season."

When the word "gun" crossed his lips, Phillip's blood chilled. He quickly ran to the cabinet that held the collection of rifles and shotguns he had accumulated through the years. He gasped when he saw the doors were open and hurriedly checked the inventory.

"He's got his old Winchester 30-30, and there's an open box of shells!"

Allen drove eastward in his Taurus. Martha, her husband, and two teenagers headed up the grassy hill behind the house toward the logging road. As Phillip started his Blazer to drive west he frantically searched his mind for the most obvious place his dad might go. Suddenly he recalled something that clicked with logic.

Through the two summers that James had resided with his eldest son, he accompanied the family whenever a trip was made to town for errands. Phillip had taken note of one particular spot on the route where his dad would sometimes perk up. It was an area where two peninsulas of woods met and were divided by the highway. It was a natural "funnel" for the deer to travel and cross the road with the least amount of exposure. He recalled that whenever they drove through that area and deer were spotted, his dad seemed to light up like a Christmas tree. It was as if the sight triggered something familiar, and for a moment a certain joy returned to the old man. Nowhere else on the journey to town did these sightings occur. Phillip confidently said to himself as he pulled out of the driveway, "Where's my dad? I know exactly where he is!"

Sure enough, as he topped a small rise in the highway and looked into the distance, there was James. The S-10 was parked on the shoulder and the old hunter was standing at the fence 30 yards or so off the road. Phillip pulled in behind the S-10, turned off the motor, and sadly stared at his dad for about a minute. His eyes were soaked with tears as he exited his vehicle and walked through the high grass to his father's side.

"Seen anything, Dad?"

Much to Phillip's surprise James responded. "Sure did, Son!"

The old man pointed to a spot about 75 yards into the thin line of timber. There among the leaves Phillip saw the hump of fur and the distinct white color of a deer's tail.

"Dad! You killed a deer!" It was not a question but a statement.

"A buck, son. It's a buck!"

Phillip was overwhelmed with the many details of the incident that had just taken place. One, his ailing, nearly mute father had spoken coherently for the first time in a long while. Second, his dad had used the word "son." It had been too many months since he had heard himself referred to by such a precious title. Third, there was a dead deer belonging to an unlicensed hunter. Fourth, it was killed on property without permission to do so. And fifth, the gun was fired from a public highway.

As Phillip assimilated the fine points it occurred to him that the place where his dad stood holding the warm, ancient, lever-action rifle was an area that once hosted the feet of a much younger hunter. The woods were not divided by pavement and barbed wire back many years ago. James had known about the whitetail "honey hole" since his mid-teens. As far as he was concerned, there was nothing at all questionable about what he had just done.

Then the son, rattled by the turn of events, thought of some things that allowed him to relax. First, his dad was not required to be licensed because of his age. And regarding the permission to shoot a deer on the property in question, Phillip knew he would simply have to beg for mercy.

After completing the necessary mental calisthenics required to calm down, Phillip was able to rejoice that he had his dad back in his care. He put his arm around the frail shoulders of his old deer-slayer and said, "Let's go see what you bagged, Pop!"

With a foot pushing down on one strand of barbed wire and pulling up on another with his hands, Phillip coached his dad through the fence and then climbed over. The two of them crunched through the dry leaves toward the buck. As they neared the lifeless body of the animal Phillip's eyes widened in surprise. The rack of antlers towered above the height of the big-bodied deer that lay on its side.

James knelt by the huge trophy and laid his gun on its ribs. "Is this mine?" he asked.

"Yes, sir. You brought down this big guy. It's yours, Dad. Way to go!"

Phillip grabbed the right main beam of the buck's antlers, held it up, and started counting. "One...two...three...four...five...six...seven...eight." At that moment his voice got higher and louder. "Nine...ten...eleven...*twelve!*" He looked at his dad as he carefully laid the massive set of antlers back to the ground. "Dad! You got yourself a 12-pointer. This is unbelievable. I am amazed!" As his son bragged on his unexpected exploit, James felt the warmth of salty tears running down his cheeks.

"This buck means a lot to me, Son. I never thought I'd get to do this again." With that humble confession, James returned to mostly silence.

The siblings gathered on the highway in response to Phillip's cellphone call. By then he was dragging the deer through the fence. The small crowd that had gathered on the road was unanimously grateful to see that the old man was safe again. And for certain, everyone was quite impressed with the 12-pointer. To this day, few have ever been seen like it in that area.

With the buck loaded into the S-10, Phillip helped his frail dad into the passenger's seat and then climbed in under the wheel. Allen drove the Blazer, and James sat across from Phillip in the small truck and stared straight ahead as if he were a child in trouble. Phillip also stared forward as if he were a parent trying to figure out what to say to a child caught in serious mischief. And, in fact, that's exactly what the two men had become.

About halfway home, as the two of them bounced on the seats of the truck, they simultaneously turned around and looked at the big buck in the bed behind them. Then they looked at each other for a long moment. As their eyes locked, Phillip saw something in his dad's expression that tore at him. He saw a look of clear understanding. For a fleeting instant it seemed his dad "knew" that in a matter of minutes the whole affair would be forgotten. Before it could happen, James offered his son the words that only the eyes can say: "Goodbye. I love you, Son."

Phillip felt the sobs welling up inside, but, for his dad's sake, he forced them back. Instead, he just returned a grateful smile to his old father. As he turned his face homeward, he thought to himself, *At least it will be a long goodbye.*

My response to this story was a prayer uttered deep in my heart:

> Dear Lord, I know time will injure my joints, weaken my muscles, and tear down the walls of my resistance to sickness. That's what time does. It beats us up like a schoolyard bully. I know I will eventually lose the fight. But, Lord, until the end, please allow me to keep my memories. I pray for James and all the others whose minds have been so ruthlessly plundered by "the thief." May You give them comfort. And give strength to those who love and care for them. I do earnestly plead, though, let me keep the memories. And, please, may my children never have to ask, "Where's Dad?"

It was last spring during turkey season that I wrote the following song. I was on my way home from an exciting hunt and was enjoying the fresh memory of it when I suddenly recalled James and the emotions I felt when I heard his story. This lyric is not presented to dredge up the intense sadness that is felt by the loved ones of Alzheimer victims. Instead, it is written so that those of us untouched by the disease can get a glimpse of the depth of loss these folks bravely face.

The Long Goodbye

Every now and then
A moment from his past
Goes dancing through his mind
And it makes him laugh

But mostly he sits quiet
In the safety of his chair
In his mind he's on a journey
But we don't know where

And he seems so far away
When we hold his hand
And he's somewhere in the distance
When he comes by me and stands

Oh, but every now and then
He looks me in the eyes
As if to say he knows
It's the long goodbye[8]

16

Number-One Arrow

Whenever the month of July rolls around there is a switch that is flipped to the "on" position somewhere in my being. It opens the circuit to a whole array of signals that bring to life the mechanisms inside me designed to pursue the elusive whitetail deer. As if on a timer, at 12:01 A.M. on the first day of the middle month of summer my mind begins to search through my memory banks for the whereabouts of the items I will need to use during the coming archery season.

My quest leads me to the shed out back where there are large, clear, plastic bags that contain the camo I will need to wash with unscented soap, let dry in the sun, and store again in bags of old leaves I saved from the year before. Also hanging securely on nails above them are my portable treestands that need to be sprayed off and aired out to free them from the smell of gasoline fumes from my mowers.

Then, with great care, I will remove my winterized compound from its case, readjust the tension on the limbs, check all the screws and hinges, cams, cables, rest, and sight pins. Then I will examine the nocking points for tightness, make sure the peep sight is unobstructed, and then wax the string. Once it is determined that the bow is in good working order, I will go back to the shed and dig out my "bag of rags," perhaps the ugliest range target that ever received a piercing.

I will then carry my bow and arrows to the area of the backyard that everyone in the Chapman household knows not to approach when I am practicing. There I will exhale a deep breath of excitement as I get ready to pull the string to full draw for the first time in much too long. And the enjoyable journey to opening morning of season begins.

Summer preparation is a treasured ritual for me. It's a time of year when I let my mind wander into the future and enjoy the fantasies of how my pulse will rise and my senses heighten as the leaves begin to fall. And for a bowhunter whose desire for the heart-stopping excitement of seeing a takeable deer has not been satisfied for several months, July is a timely reprieve. It is the medicine needed to regulate an advanced case of acute buck fever.

As the season draws very near, around mid-September, my preparation for opening day intensifies. By this time I am a walking heap of anxious anticipation. I start to focus on the fine points of readiness like adding a small drop of vegetable oil, which has no telltale scent, to certain moving parts of my bow and remarking the adjustment straps on my treestand with bright paint that can be more easily seen in the pale light of dawn.

The very last detail I usually cover is something I consider incredibly important—so much so that I do it with a great deal of deliberation. It is the process of choosing my number-one arrow. I don't care at all to go into the woods on the first morning of archery season with less than full confidence in the flight and accuracy of my "string bullets." Nothing can dampen the high hopes of a successful hunt quicker than not knowing exactly how and where an arrow is going to sail once it leaves the bow. After weeks and months of scouting and practicing, not to mention the expense, why mess up the moment of truth with a less than total feeling of assurance that all systems are go.

Knowing I will mount only four arrows to my quiver, I begin the painstaking process of selection. With "spin checks" already out of the way and the undesirable shafts culled out, I reduce the number of possibilities to a dozen. Then I replace all damaged plastic fletching. After that I shoot each one at least a dozen times. As they leave the bow I watch them fly. Amazingly, even though they look and feel precisely the same from one to the next, the arrows have their own character. Once I have picked out six arrows that seem to excel in terms of flight quality, I start the process again. When I am down to four arrows that have convinced me they are "aces in my air force," I then begin a very discriminatory search for the one that will get the honorable position of top gun.

At this point I put the broadheads on the arrows. Knowing the three thin blades might slightly alter the way an arrow will fly, I go back to step one and start shooting each shaft at least a dozen times, one after the other, at a target specially made for broadheads. I try to observe how the arrow slides off the rest as well as any unusual or excessive movements it might make such as fishtailing or porpoising.

Each year I have found that one arrow seems to rise above all the others when it comes to performance. Its consistency at flying to the spot my sight pin covers is noticeable, and its behavior during release feels right. Three other excellent flyers are chosen as alternates. I then take my Scripto permanent ink pen and mark the odd color vein on each shaft with their rank. I start with last of the group and write: "#4" and the year of the season. Then I mark number three and two. At that point I stop.

As I hold the arrow in my hand that I consider to be the best among all the rest, I always feel a little melancholy. I think to myself, *This is the one I will depend on to do the job. This "faithful friend" has consistently shown it is worthy of occupying the first slot in my quiver. I will protect it, and from this point on I will limit its testing to one shot per day just to make sure it is still number one.* With that, I mark it, set it aside, and continue my wait for opening morning.

This tedious process has not been fruitless. I have collected a good number of arrows that are either bent or broken—but they are also covered with dried blood! On most of those successful shafts are plastic veins with markings that read, "#1." If I am fortunate enough to find them after they are used to take a deer, I never throw them away. Somewhere among all my souvenirs from seasons past are the remains of these "top guns." They are like old soldiers who are retired and deserve a safe resting place.

One day as I was going through some hunting memorabilia in my garage, I found a former #1 that had been slightly bent as a result of an encounter with a whitetail's rib. It had been put away for memory's sake and it still held its "#1" badge written in black on the bright orange vein. I held it for a moment and recalled with joy the particular hunt that it represented. Then I whispered a familiar compliment: ("Well done, thou good and faithful servant.") As if the arrow had become a mirror in my hands, I held it up to eye level and asked, "What about me? Am I a number-one arrow?"

The question was loaded with an abundance of implications. As I pondered it, I thought about my life as a husband and dad. I couldn't help but wonder, "Is my behavior in the presence of my family displaying the straightness of important virtues like honesty, integrity, and devotion? Am I worthy to be their leader?" It was a sobering moment of self-examination.

I then thought of even more serious questions. ("As a man who claims to belong to Christ, am I a servant He could hold in His hands and confidently write on my heart, as He has done on others through the ages, the inscription '#1'? Could He trust me to do whatever He asks of me? And if I'm called upon to be launched at only one target, am I willing to be bent and broken for that single cause?")

These were questions that gripped my emotions that day. (They inspired me to reassess my willingness to be tested. I wondered if I would ever make the mistake of being satisfied to be less than the best I could be in His hands.) As I allowed the impact of the analogy to continue its work in my heart, I thought of what I sometimes do to turn an aluminum arrow that is a little wobbly into one that flies with greater stability. From time to time a careful spin test will reveal the shaft is straight but the broadhead is sitting just off center, taking away its ability to spin perfectly. To correct this problem I have to apply heat to the area where the screw-in insert is mounted to the shaft. After the glue melts it allows me to adjust the broadhead and then spin test it once more. If needed, the flame is applied again and again until the adjustments result in an arrow that spins without the slightest waver.

This corrective technique is a vivid picture of what the Lord often does to His own arrows. When He needs to readjust us, He applies the heat. In 1 Peter 4:12, we face the news that each of us should "not be surprised at the fiery ordeal among you, which comes upon you for your testing, as though some strange thing were happening to you." God works on us because He loves us and wants to help us "straighten up and fly right." The flame He applies can come in the form of anything from persecution by an evil world to a close family member who grates on our patience. And just as I have to heat and reheat my metal arrows, He will take us to His workbench as often as needed. Why? Because He needs us to be in the best condition when our divine moment of truth arrives. To be less than an accurate arrow for Him would be a sad waste of life.

When all is said and done and those I love hold the memory of me in their hands, perhaps in the form of a picture or something written on paper, I deeply long for them to be able to say, "He was a good one. He 'flew' well!"

More importantly, may I strive to be faithful in allowing God to test me the way He wills in order to make me more effective for His purposes. In order for the right adjustments to be accomplished in my life, I know I must allow Him to examine me in the way Psalm 139 puts it: "Search me, O God, and know my heart; try me and know my anxious thoughts; and see if there be any hurtful way in me, and lead me in the everlasting way."

Not by any means in a haughty attitude nor with a wish to outdo another, I want to be one of God's number-one arrows. Someday I want to hear *Him* say, "Well done, thou good and faithful servant" (KJV). That lofty goal is one only He can help me meet. I know this to be true because of the benediction found in Jude 24: "Now to Him who is able to keep you from stumbling, and to make you stand in the presence of His glory blameless with great joy, to the only God our Savior, through Jesus Christ our Lord, be glory, majesty, dominion and authority, before all time and now and forever. Amen."

May each of us be willing to let Him do what it takes to test us, adjust us, and write on our hearts "#1 servant."

Lyric Credits

1. Bring That Child to Me, Steve Chapman/Dawn Treader Music/BMI, on "An Evening Together," S&A Family, Inc., SA-3000.

2. Father's Embrace, Steve Chapman/Times & Seasons Music/BMI, on "Family Favorites," S&A Family, Inc., SACD-105.

3. Mama's Brave Prayer, Steve Chapman/Times & Seasons Music/BMI, on "The Silver Bridge," S&A Family, Inc., SACD-97.

4. Wednesday's Prayer, Steve Chapman/Times & Seasons Music/BMI, on "At the Potter's House," S&A Family, Inc., SACD-110. This lyric is also featured in a pocket-sized book entitled *Wednesday Prayer—A Father's Guide to Praying & Fasting for His Children* (1999, S&A Family, Inc.).

5. Daddy's Shoes, Steve Chapman/Times & Seasons Music/BMI, 1999.

6. Crosses on Highways, Steve Chapman/Times & Seasons Music/BMI, 1999, on "This House Still Stands," 2000.

7. When I Walk These Fields, Steve Chapman/Times & Seasons Music/BMI.

8. The Long Goodbye, Steve Chapman/Times & Seasons Music/BMI, 1999, on "This House Still Stands," 2000.

About the Author

Proudly claiming West Virginia as his home state, Steve Chapman grew up as the son of a preacher. He met his wife, Annie, in junior high school in 1963. In March of 1975, they married after dating a few months and settled in Nashville, Tennessee There they have raised their son and daughter, Nathan and Heidi.

Steve is president of S&A Family, Inc., an organization formed to oversee the production of the Chapman's recorded music. They have had "family life" as the theme of their lyrics since they began singing together in 1980. As Dove Award-winning artists, their schedule sends them to over 100 cities a year to present concerts that feature songs from over 15 recorded projects.

Steve's love of hunting began in his early teens on a weekend when one of his dad's church members invited him to tag along on an October squirrel hunt. Archery is his first choice for use in the field, followed by muzzle loader, and then pistol or rifle. To date, according to Steve's calculations, he has entered the woods before daylight on at least a thousand mornings. He says he hopes for just as many more.

As a member of API's pro-staff team, Steve uses and endorses API treestands.

Steve and Annie's Discography

This House Still Stands
At the Potter's House
Never Turn Bacck
Chapters
Waiting to Hear
Mother's Touch
Tools for the Trade
Family Favorites
Kiss of Hearts
An Evening Together
The Silver Bridge

Books by Steve and Annie Chapman

A Look at Life from a Deer Stand (Steve)
Putting Anger in Its Place (Annie)
What a Hunter Brings Home (Steve)

---

*For a list of available products (CDs/cassettes/videos/books)
or more information about the Chapmans
please write to:*

S&A Family, Inc.
P.O. Box 535
Madison, TN 37116

Or check out their website:
www.steveandanniechapman.com

Other Good
Harvest House Reading

A Look at Life from a Deer Stand
Steve Chapman

Taking you on his successful and not-so-successful hunts, Steve Chapman shares his skills for successful hunting—and living. With excitement and humor, he shares the parallels between hunting and walking with God.

The Ultimate Hunt
Jim Grassi

Internationally known outdoorsman Jim Grassi reveals how hunters can experience God's love more deeply. Through hunting adventures—and misadventures—Grassi invites you to begin your spiritual journey to the soul of creation: God's heart.

A Father for All Seasons
Bob Welch

Bob Welch takes a joyful and contemplative look at the lifelong love between fathers and sons. Welch reflects on his own experiences and shares the everyday journeys of others in this collection of stories that is rich with humor, wisdom, and spiritual truths.